# SAY IT LIKE IT IS

## Entitlement, political correctness and the demise of common sense

**by**

**Dave Sampson**

authorHOUSE®

*AuthorHouse™*
*1663 Liberty Drive, Suite 200*
*Bloomington, IN 47403*
*www.authorhouse.com*
*Phone: 1-800-839-8640*

*First published by AuthorHouse   12/5/2007*

*Printed in the United States of America
Bloomington, Indiana*

*This book is printed on acid-free paper.*

*ISBN: 978-1-4343-0576-3 (sc)*

*Cover photo taken by Jill Law (kokographix@charter.net)*

# CONTENTS

# INTRODUCTION

Welcome to the wonderful world of political correctness. A world where niceties trump truth and where feel good phrases confuse our perception of reality.

It's not been until recently that our society has been influenced by the implementation of political correctness. Until just thirty or forty years ago, Americans were not only allowed to speak truthfully and directly, they were expected to. Thanks to Liberals and their social experiments, the American public hardly remembers the days when true and direct speech was the norm. To even say we used to, "Call a spade a spade" is considered highly offensive in today's P.C. world. Let's just say that P.C. speech has rounded the edges of reality and has warmed and softened the cold hard truth. It is a necessary step in the Liberal's plan to implement tolerance, acceptance and their perception of equality. It's as dangerous to our nation as a terrorist attack, but has been implemented slowly over the decades and is now commonly accepted as the norm.

Political correctness has given us words like, "Undocumented worker" and demonized the label, "Illegal alien." It requires us to be acceptant of these hard working "Migrants" and respectful of their culture, customs, religion and heritage. Anyone not totally acceptant of those who have invaded our country against the law, are labeled bigots and called prejudiced and intolerant. Political correctness at its best.

Political correctness allows terrorists in America the right to legal council while groups like the ACLU defend terrorist actions. The P.C. world in which we live has made stating the truth an act of cruelty. Using common sense and human intuition to racially profile individuals in the name of national security and self-preservation has become not just highly offensive, but illegal. Political correctness has taught us to think we're all the same regardless of our differences. It dictates we condemn achievers and commend underachievers.

Political correctness finds us providing assistance to every American who requests it, but also aid to every foreign nation who tells us they need it. To gain acceptance in the "Global community," the U.S. provides funds and food to every nation on the planet that experiences a natural or man-made disaster. This includes sending billions of dollars to enemy nations whose sole purpose for existence is to murder Americans and destroy our way of life. To be politically correct, we ignore the fact that these nations hate us and wish to do us harm. Instead, we commit to providing aid each and every time an earthquake rocks Iran or a flood occurs in communist China. Isn't that nice? The fact that we offer aid never changes the opinion of communists, terrorists or Muslim extremists, but Liberals in this country hope that will someday change. According to

Liberals, it's politically correct to want the respect of deranged Jihadists and murderers.

From political correctness we go to the wonderful world of entitlement. A world where the government is not only expected, but obligated to provide its citizens with any and all things required to insure an individuals survival and happiness.

Let's admit it. There are so many freebies in today's society that to many Americans the mere suggestion of self-sufficiency seems callous and cruel. The sudden elimination, or even drastic reduction, of these social programs would bring a screeching halt to life as we know it. You and I are so used to hearing about public assistance programs that we've become deaf to what those words actually mean and numb to the effects that they have on those who "Benefit" from them.

Welfare! It comes in many forms, encompasses entire sections of our population and has evolved into big, big business. Food stamps, subsidized housing, free medical care, free childcare, cash benefits, disaster relief, reduced or free school meals, free summer lunches. All of these programs and many more have been instituted by "Caring" bureaucrats over the years and have grown, predictably, year after year. In fact, it is incomprehensible to even suggest a planned reduction of these entitlements that, for the most part, promote dependency and breed apathy. Those who have stood up and suggested that it's time to promote individual responsibility and break the cycle of poverty created by social programs are called racist, insensitive, intolerant or uncompassionate. How dare anyone try to separate a comfortably low-income individual from his or her free monthly entitlements. How dare anyone suggest that by removing free services to able but apathetic persons, we might actually be doing them a favor by "Nudging" them into supporting themselves. How dare anyone suggests to bureaucrats that we cut the government fat that inevitably surrounds any and all programs aimed at helping Americas "Underprivileged."

There's more to a job than a paycheck. It may sound clichéd but it's so very true. By getting up and out to work and supporting ones self, a person gains not only monetarily but also develops pride, self-respect and a sense of self worth. These things, even more than a check on the first and fifteenth, are why every able-bodied individual in the country should work. It doesn't matter if your job requires you to ask, "Would you like fries with that," or say "Yes, Mr. President."

Anybody who says it like it is, is seen as mean and cruel and evil. That being said, this mean, cruel and evil individual is going to stick his neck out and say what needs to be said. If it offends somebody or ruffles feathers or makes a Liberal gasp, so be it.

It's time to require Americans to be self-sufficient again. It's time to shed the entitlement mentality we've been progressively forced to adopt. It's time to let the private sector

(Community groups, churches, philanthropic foundations, service organizations and caring individuals) do what they have always done better than government, and that would be to take care of family, friends and those in need of assistance.

# CHAPTER 1
# NATURAL DISASTERS

Let's start out by acknowledging that natural disasters are just that, natural disasters. They're not the result of an evil government plot to eradicate any specific race or region. They're not generated by a secret underground "Weather Creation Lab" to be set loose on citizens of America or any other country in the world. Natural disasters occur naturally. Contrary to some current popular beliefs, natural disasters are not specific to the poor areas of our country. I know it creates a great uproar to blame natural disasters on a political party that you don't like, or on a race that differs from your own, but that just isn't the case. Lets stick to the facts.

Natural Disasters occur on every continent on earth. They range from earthquakes, floods and tsunamis, to tornadoes, hurricanes and plagues. Fires and volcanic eruptions are considered "Acts of God" and not acts of George W. Bush. Some natural disasters we are able to predict and prepare for, while others are so sudden they happen in a instant or a few seconds, with no warning at all. All natural disasters bring with them the potential for death and destruction. The severity of the damage they cause depends on the scale, duration and size of their power, and also on the population of the region in which they occur.

Natural disasters have occurred throughout earth's history. They are nothing new and they will continue long after you and I are gone. Also, regardless of what the entire click of environmental nuts say, the disasters we've seen recently are not the result of human-caused global warming. Does global warming occur? Sure it does. There's proof throughout history that global temperatures rise and fall creating both ice ages and global thaws. Let's not be so conceited and pompous that we actually give ourselves credit as humans, for the effects of global warming. It's been occurring naturally for billions of years.

Where does the topic of Natural disasters coincide with the idea of entitlement? If you've been anywhere but in a closet for the past couple of years you've seen the news stories blaming the government for slow response time to these disasters. You've heard about the trillions of dollars that our government has dedicated to rebuilding cities and towns affected by these events. You've heard the blame put on the government for the suffering of individuals inside these disaster zones. In all of these stories, who is blamed? The government! Why? Because all personal responsibility has been removed from our society. Therefore, it can be nobody but the government's fault for the results caused by natural disasters. Let's look at some facts.

The Federal Emergency Management Agency (FEMA) has a list of the top 10 natural disasters that have had an affect on the United States. (The amounts in dollars below reflect the amount obligated from the President's Disaster Relief Fund for FEMA's assistance programs. The actual total costs of rebuilding were far higher). Amazingly, *all* top ten events have taken place between 1989 and today. This is simply because FEMA rates its disasters on the amount of financial damage that they cause. Of course this top 10 list won't include any truly devastating earthquakes or fires from the early 1900's, the killer Indonesian volcanic eruptions in the 1800's, or any other catastrophic event that occurred prior to 1989. The environmentalists look at the fact that FEMA lists the top 10 natural disasters (Which have taken place in the past 15 years) as proof that humans are causing these events to be more frequent and more severe. Never do they break down the reasons why FEMA categorizes these events at the top 10. As we know, FEMA rates disasters on the financial damage that disasters cause. We all know that the Alaskan earthquake (and ensuing tsunami) that violently shook our northernmost state in 1964 was a severe quake, but because it occurred in an isolated location and only affected a small amount of individuals and structures, it's not even close to a top

10 event. The 1906 San Francisco earthquake and fires that caused the destruction of the majority of "The City by the Bay," is referred to as one of the biggest natural disasters of modern time. Yet it isn't listed on FEMA's list of top 10 disasters. Why? Although the majority of San Francisco needed to be rebuilt, the cost to do so in the early 1900's was a fraction of what it cost to make repairs to isolated parts of the city following the 1989 quake. Thus, it's not a top 10 contender.

Some of the most financially devastating natural disasters have occurred in some of the most populated areas of the southeast. According to the Census Bureau, Florida is a state of over 17 million individuals. There are numerous major cities, theme parks and hundreds of communities throughout the state. Florida also happens to be smack-dab in the middle of the annual hurricane zone. It makes sense that seven out of FEMA's top 10 disasters were hurricanes and tropical storms that affected Florida. The nature of these storms, with heavy rains and damaging winds, are the reason they constitute such a high percentage of the top 10 natural disasters. The fact that people have located and developed in the path of these storms is the reason why they cause the most financial damage. Only one *storm* listed in the top ten during the past decade and a half has missed Florida. One!

So eight of the top ten natural disasters (numbers 2-9) in the past 15 years were tropical storms or their big brother, the hurricane. What are the other two and where did they rank? Number 10 was the flood in 1993 that affected Midwestern states from North Dakota and Wisconsin to Kansas and Missouri. Warm temperatures and heavy rains following wet snow caused severe flooding which wiped out towns and farms on a huge scale. The cost of the floods was estimated at 1.14 billion dollars.

What topped the list? Number one on FEMA's list was California's 1994 Northridge earthquake. At 4:30 am on January 17th 1994 the earth shook 20 miles Northwest of Los Angeles. The 6.7 quake was far from the most severe quake California has felt. In fact several stronger quakes had been recorded in less populated areas just a few years prior to the Northridge quake. The reason why this disaster ranked number one was because it struck where humans had settled and developed. California's population of nearly 36 million is several times larger than many small countries in the world. Los Angeles County alone has a population of 10 million. Due to the location of the quake, the population density and infrastructure required to accommodate that number of people, the Northridge quake caused the most financial damage prior to 2005's Hurricane Katrina. The estimated cost was 6.7 billion dollars.

We know the cost for the number one and the number ten disasters as listed by FEMA. What was the cost of all those hurricanes that ranked between two and nine? Combined they were estimated to cost 13.8 billion dollars.

If we look at the ten deadliest US natural Disasters we find that number one deadliest was a hurricane in Galveston Texas in 1900. This monster hurricane claimed 8,000 lives. The aforementioned San Francisco earthquake of 1906 claimed 700 lives and ranks as the third deadliest in US history. Numerous other tornadoes and hurricanes dot the top ten list claiming between 255 and 720 lives per event.

On a worldwide scale the death toll resulting from natural disasters is astronomical. Chinese floods have claimed the lives of millions. Volcanoes in Indonesia have killed hundreds of thousands over the past few centuries. Earthquakes in countries situated around the Pacific Ring of Fire have caused death and destruction to thousands upon thousands of people.

Regardless of how we break down the numbers, we know natural disasters are costly in both dollars and in human life. We also have a pretty good idea of where, if not when, these disasters are likely to occur. Statistically Florida, Louisiana, North Carolina, South Carolina and Mississippi are likely to get pounded by at least one major hurricane every year. In most cases these states will face multiple tropical storms and hurricanes in a given year. States in the mid-west's "Tornado alley" are guaranteed to get blasted by several if not dozens of tornadoes during tornado season. Kentucky, Tennessee, Missouri, Iowa, Minnesota, Illinois, Nebraska,

Okalahoma, Arkansas, Texas, and Indiana are all prime targets to get hit by severe tornadoes each spring.

Houses that are built in the flood plains of the Mississippi and Missouri rivers, as well as any other rivers that flood regularly, are bound to be soaked by floodwaters sooner or later. The Pacific Northwest poses a bigger threat of volcanic activity than anywhere else in the country. Should we be surprised when Mt Saint Helens blows again? What if California's Mt. Shasta began showing signs of awaking from dormancy? Would you buy a house at the mountain's base, because it was pretty?

If we must continue stating the obvious then I guess I'll tell you that those who live where it rains are bound to get wet and those living in snow zones will inevitably get snowed on. Kids who touch the hot burner will get burned, but unlike the federal government the kid will learn from his mistake. It only takes once for a small child to learn. Why does a huge government never learn? What am I talking about? Let's recall the events that comprised the 2005 hurricane season. A record number of tropical storms were named in '05. Several large storms hit America's shorelines from Florida to Texas. As with most natural disasters, everywhere the hurricanes hit, disaster struck and chaos ensued.

Hurricane Katrina demonstrated to us all the incredibly dependent behavior displayed by residents of Louisiana and Mississippi. Dependent on the government for food and shelter, large parts of the population in those two states are poor. Evacuation warnings given three and four days prior to the storm were not heeded. Instead, many residents vowed to stay in their homes regardless of the desperate predictions of disaster. Few who stayed took the precautions needed to survive such a devastating storm. It wasn't until after the August 29th, category 4 hurricane hit the gulf coast, that folks decided it might be smart to stock up on food and water to see them through. By then it was too late and the fault for being unprepared had to be shifted to somebody. Enter the federal government.

It wasn't until a few days after the initial shock of the damage caused by Katrina, that the blame game started. Initially it was a low rumble of questions stirred by the Bush Administration's opponents. "Why did it take so long to get to the survivors, even though the roads were destroyed, the power was out and there was eight feet of water covering everything in sight?" That low rumble quickly gained momentum, as well as volume, as the media, Black leaders and government dependants started putting blame on the government at local, state and especially federal levels. All of a sudden it was President Bush's fault that residents of New Orleans didn't evacuate. According to Screwy Louie Farrakhan, it was Bush and Cheney who planted explosives at the base of the levees to sabotage their integrity. Screwy Louie also accused the federal government of intentionally delaying their response in order to kill off the poor Black population of

Louisiana. Although these claims are as ridiculous as they are untrue, they should be expected. For years the federal government has provided for the poor residents of Louisiana and Mississippi. The government has seen to their basic needs and has told them that they'd be taken care of. Now, in the face of disaster, big brother wasn't there to take care of them. Whose fault is that? Well these poor, indigent folks can't be expected to take care of themselves. In fact the government has all but stripped their ability to do so.

Apparently, the poor residents of the affected states were unable to listen to weather reports, public evacuation warnings, and predictions of disaster, too. They couldn't get to the local store a week before the hurricane to stock up on the five-day supply of food, water and necessities as recommended by their government leaders. They heeded no advise for survival given by their government.

In fact they'd just as soon ignore "The man" as save their own hides. So why *wouldn't* they blame this predicament on the government, same as they do any other? And why *not* use the chaos caused by the destructive storm to loot local shops and stores. We did see some people coming out of grocery stores with canned food and bottled water but we saw even more exiting with television sets being carried out of electronic stores. Tennis shoes and sweat suits were exiting sporting goods stores quicker than kindergarteners in a fire drill. High dollar items of all types were taken from any and all stores unlucky enough to be in the path of a determined looter. This behavior too was blamed on the government. "My Heart Will Go On" crooner and Canadian citizen Celine Dion was interviewed and said that the looters deserved all they got because they've had to go without those items for so long. Are we to assume that it's the government's fault that these folks didn't have top-dollar electronics and clothes? Apparently there's no other conclusion to draw but that the American government just doesn't provide enough Nike shoes and flat screen televisions to its poor citizens.

Expectant leaders at the local and state levels also blamed the federal government for their own lack of competence. Governors and mayors who dropped the ball in the evacuation process took the focus off their miserable planning failures prior to the disaster by pointing fingers at George Bush and the National Guard for a so called slow response, following it. If there's no accountability from local leadership how can anyone expect citizens to be accountable? Again, we see displayed the total lack of personal responsibility learned by those reliant on the government. It's ridiculous yes, but it's predictable and should have been expected.

Now lets move onto the bigger issue of rebuilding a city that is situated on a coastline, below a large lake, in the direct path of annual hurricanes and lies below sea level. Sounds like a good plan to me. Let's throw billions of dollars and millions of man-hours into rebuilding a city that will inevitably be completely destroyed again. It may happen next year or it may happen in ten years but it *will* happen again. How many times has the government thrown huge amounts of money to rebuild the exact same parts of Florida? It seems to me that if there's a pattern of weather that causes mass destruction to specific areas, and the numerous rebuilding of that area does nothing to change the destructive weather, then maybe it's not a good idea to continue to rebuild there. Sound logical to anybody else? How many times do we need to burn our hands before we quit touching the hot stove?

As long as the federal government spends billions to rebuild houses, towns, cities and infrastructure, people will continue to move back into those destruction zones. After years of the government whipping out the nation's checkbook, following any and all natural disasters, people have begun to not only expect cash, but have also begun to bitch about the amount they get and how fast it's received.

I'm pretty sure that if insurance and the government didn't cover the cost to rebuild these folks' homes, and they were responsible for paying all costs from site preparation to construction to landscaping to interior decoration, it would only take one total loss of property for "Hurricane zone" Americans to learn their lesson about the futility of challenging Mother Nature. *Challenge* is the active word here. From those who lost their homes, to local and state government officials, to the president of the United States, the common message following a destructive hurricane or massive tropical storm is, "We will be strong. We will rebuild. We will work together and we will persevere!" I'll tell you what, "We're sick of hearing it!" Is there anything more pompous or ridiculous than the idea that man can control or direct storms the size of small countries? Are we really to believe that a strong will to "Persevere" can deter the next hurricane from totally destroying all that was done to rebuild?

How scary is it that those who have their houses destroyed and their lives altered by a natural disaster, rely on the very government who rebuilds in the same area where they know for a fact that those same lives will be altered and their homes destroyed again?

Some would argue that states in the hurricane zone are just a beautiful part of the country that storms hit "Occasionally". They say not developing in the hurricane zone just isn't realistic. I argue that it's just as silly to build directly in the path of hurricanes as it is to build in the Antarctic. Both are inhospitable places. The fact that the Antarctic is inhospitable year round and that Florida is only a death-zone for half the year, is inconsequential. I have yet to see a government aid program that dedicates billions of dollars to develop and inhabit the barren, frozen tundra that the Antarctic encompasses. Why then, do we continue to spend good money after bad to inhabit America's inhospitable lands?

Katrina was a great example of pissing away government money. First, we spent millions of dollars to mobilize rescues for those who ignored warnings to evacuate. They had nearly a week and countless warnings on television, on radio and in the paper. Obviously it was the talk of the town. Nevertheless, these folks knew the government would be there to pick up the pieces for their lack of responsibility, so they simply took none. Then we gave "Survivors" a government credit card loaded up with $2,000 cash. This was to be used by individuals and families to purchase food, clothing and shelter until their banks were re-opened and their government services restored. Like any other government benefit that is given instead of earned, a portion of the credit cards were used to purchase booze, lap dances at strip joints, firearms and cigarettes.

Luckily, after they blew that money, the government was able to re-institute the regular monthly benefits that these folks had relied on for years. Then the government rebuilt the levee system. The very same system that was supposed to be maintained through the years with government dollars allocated for that specific purpose. Where did those dollars go? Lost to the same corrupt politicians that are infamous for scandal in Louisiana. Then we get to the actual rebuilding of structures; houses, apartments, strip malls, bridges, ports, hotels, casinos and high-rise buildings. How many trillions of dollars will be spent on these structures? Too damn many! It's just a matter of time before another storm blows through and we do it all again. It's beginning to remind me of the Bill Murray classic, "Groundhog Day." Unlike the movie though, the government never gets it right.

Those in the Pacific Northwest the New England states, the Mid-West and even Hawaii and Alaska are paying to continually rebuild the same hurricane-hit places year after year. If volcanoes erupted as frequently as hurricanes hit the gulf coast, I'd be willing to bet that any Floridian required to pay each and every year for communities and towns built on the slopes of Mount St. Helens would be fed up by now. They might even start to wonder how smart the citizens and government of Washington really are to rebuild after being blown to bits every "Volcano season."

Americans are asked to be compassionate, and by any standard we are the most compassionate and generous people in the world. We are asked to donate to relief agencies to assist survivors and displaced victims of natural disasters and we always answer with unbelievable generosity. We're asked to assist in the rebuilding of these hard-hit communities and until now we've just said okay and done what we could do to help. But people are starting to talk and the obvious (if politically incorrect) is being said. "We'll do anything to help the victims of this great tragedy but by God, I won't spend a dime to rebuild a place destined to be home to another tragedy!" Does this make us uncaring or insensitive? I don't think so. I think it shows the courage of a minority of people to stand up and state what should be obvious to all Americans *and* their genius government leaders.

Bottom Line? Without the government there to pick up the pieces of predictable and consistent disasters, there would be far fewer disasters that would cost our government trillions of dollars. Don't get me wrong, the *disasters* would still be there but businesses and homes and people wouldn't be. Therefore, there'd be no cost to repair what isn't there to begin with. Government dependence causes the death of countless Americans each year. Without government "Help," they would have moved to safer regions long ago. I just wonder how long it'll be before some tort lawyer sues the national government for killing Americans by rebuilding their homes in disaster zones. After all, we are a litigious society. There's another thing we could blame on the Bush Administration. Not only do they conspire to create these natural disasters, they pretend to help the survivors only to keep them in danger zones in order to more easily kill them off at a later date.

It's time the government step back, look at these events and decide what priorities the nation's money should be spent on. Do we continue to waste federal dollars on the same destructive events that cannot be changed, or do we learn from the past and change our behavior to avoid the destruction? Nothing will change until a "Tough-love" approach is taken with those who insist on living in hurricane zones. Money will be flushed down the drain until the President and the President's administration put their proverbial foot down and say, "You folks are on your own the next time your homes and towns are demolished." It's time the government put some personal responsibility back on people. By doing so, you and I (Who have the brains to not live in a hurricane zone) might just see a reduction in our federal taxes. Imagine keeping more money in our paychecks because we refuse to pay to rebuild New Orleans every couple of years. All it takes is you and I demanding that the federal government use a little common sense. Mix in a little deductive reasoning and presto; we can rest assured that we'll not be held accountable for the ongoing repair costs incurred by hurricane-struck towns.

It'll never happen. Political correctness has overtaken common sense in our country. We are forced to ignore facts in order to accommodate a person's feelings. We are told to turn our back to the truth if the truth might hurt. Touchy-feely Liberals have convinced the majority of policy makers that by drawing the line and stating facts unconditionally, they risk the wrath of the voters come next election. So we're caught in the Liberals favorite quagmire, either say it like it is and lose the votes so you can't change the way things are, *or* do nothing and be re-elected year after year to see that nothing rattles the status quo. It's the old saying, "When good men do nothing" come to life. As a result, we say what is expected and then display pseudo-compassion for the "Victims" when what we really want to do is simply say it like it is and shake these folks back to reality.

## INTERNATIONAL AID

America! Respected by few, hated by many. Capitalism and a free market have ensured our place as the wealthiest and the most envied nation in the world. It has also cemented our fate as a target of the jealous and the extreme.

In an ongoing effort to appease radicals and befriend rogue nations, America spends astronomical amounts of money on nations whose governments despise us. We want to appear to the world as compassionate and caring when the world actually sees us as evil and imperialistic. Why then, do we continue to pay for natural disasters that happen half way around the world to countries that hate us? Good question! Iran is a huge threat to the United States and to the world. They have developed nuclear capabilities and have a mindset that makes them extremely dangerous to the civilized world. They refuse to dismantle weapons that could be used against us and they press forward in the development of more deadly weapons. We should be strong in our requests and swift in our action if Iran refuses to abandon their nuclear program. What do we do instead? As with most problem nations around the globe, we pussyfoot around and exhaust all avenues of diplomacy, treaties, talks and bribery before shelving the issue for later discussion. Oh yea, and we send them billions of dollars in medical aide, supplies and trained volunteers every time they have a flood or an earthquake.

While some may see this as compassionate, it garners us no respect and affords us no kindness on the behalf of nations we perpetually aid. These folks hate us and would like to wipe us off the face of the earth. They want to see our society crumble and our way of life erased. Although we receive little thanks for our efforts, I can't remember a time that the aid was turned away or refused due to a disagreement of philosophies or disapproval for the American way of life, which affords us the ability to help in the first place.

Not only does our government continue to send billions of dollars to countries around the world, the citizens of America open their wallets and purses and send millions more. The Red Cross sends out a plea for relief and we swamp them with our generous donations. Music promoters and musicians organize blowout concerts that raise huge amounts of money for relief efforts. Americans come together to provide food, water, medical supplies, volunteers and cash to thousands of natural disaster victims around the world each year. Yet our government received almost immediate criticism regarding our response to those in need in Sri Lanka and Indonesia. We were called selfish for initially offering just 350 million dollars and Bush later asked congress to up our offerings to nearly a billion dollars. The same international community that despises us and badmouths us every chance they get, is somehow able to shame us into taking the lions share of financial responsibility for the world's disasters.

Predictably and unfortunately, the world looks to the United States as a child looks to its mother for help and support every time a crisis arises. We've trained the world as Pavlov trained his dogs. The earth shakes and the U.S. hands out money. Floodwaters crest a riverbank and the U.S. hands out money. A killer wave crashes and the U.S. hands out money. As a nation, we've put ourselves in this position and it's time we get ourselves out of the role of worldwide financier. But as we've seen with any other entitlement program we've ever instituted, it's almost impossible to reign in once it's been established.

In 2003, the United States spent 16.25 billion dollars on foreign disaster aid. That equates to nearly double the amount spent by the next most generous nation, Japan. If you include debt forgiveness, the U.S. figure rises to twenty four billion dollars. It's estimated that each American is paying thirteen cents per day for foreign aid. Each American donates, on average, another five cents a day. This adds up rapidly when you consider the number of citizens in the country. Yet it's never enough. Critics call America stingy and complain that we should be doing much more to assist poorer nations in times of need. Foreign nations grab the money we offer then criticize us for our lack of generosity.

Why do we allow ourselves to be persuaded by nations who show us no respect? What we ought to do is send donated funds raised by concerned Americans and nothing else. Anybody can easily put themselves in the place of a victim of a natural disaster. It is the American way to help whenever possible and the generosity we show is overwhelming. While you and I are happy to open or checkbooks to ease the suffering of victims of natural disasters in China, India, or Afghanistan, we can't allow our government to give away the farm. It's not the responsibility of politicians to commit our country's money to the rebuilding of wells in a third-world country. It may sound cruel but the truth of the matter is this; charity begins at home.

It is utterly obvious to patriotic Americans that wars need to be fought preemptively and on foreign soil. It is equally obvious that natural disaster victims need to be cared for in America first and even then, only for so long and with certain common sense stipulations. America is running in deficit mode. Liberals constantly bitch about the cost of war and of keeping our nation secure but never have I heard them bitch about sending too much money to a humanitarian interest. Hell, they'd be willing to take on ten times our current national deficit if that money was guaranteed to be used to help other people in other countries. Mention defense though, and watch them turn all shades of red trying to stop further spending on the safety and security of our country.

Keeping the wheels of international politics greased is understandable. Simply giving away billions of America's tax dollars in a feeble attempt to buy respect and a favorable outlook of foreign nations that despise us…It's just stupid.

It is said that, "You can please some of the people some of the time but you can't please all of the people all of the time." It's about time we quit trying. America became a strong nation by ensuring that our morals, military and society were strong. Now we attempt to appease our friends and enemies instead of continuing to strengthen our own country. I expect this will not change. In fact, Liberals are working hard to further this situation and if not stopped, America will pay dearly as a result.

# Chapter 2
# Happiness. An Entitlement?

...And the right to pursue happiness... What a great country. One that allows and ensures that its citizens can do whatever they want to gain personal happiness (within the law of course.) That means if money makes you happy, you can get an education and work in a profession that pays well. If charity work makes you happy, you can establish your own non-profit that helps whomever or whatever you wish to help, or you can work for an already established charity. If serving your country makes you happy, you have the freedom of deciding which branch of the military best fits your expectations. If your happiness comes from farming you can buy your own private land and raise crops to your heart's content. If happiness is family then by all means get married and have as many kids as you can responsibly raise. Opportunities abound and happiness is there for the taking, yet to some that isn't enough. Like food, shelter and other basic needs, some individuals want happiness handed to them on a silver platter. Ever since Roosevelt introduced the New Deal, Americans have become more expectant and more demanding of entitlement programs. Society in general has an entitlement mentality in which citizens feel that they are owed. Our government has nurtured that mentality by proving that if you demand loud and long enough, you'll receive whatever it is you're demanding. Much like a baby who's picked up each time it fusses, Americans are coddled and provided for in ways our founding fathers never intended. It's made us dependent and progressively less able to support ourselves. But I digress.

The only catch to pursuing happiness is *you* have to pursue it! It can't be handed to you in an envelope or on a silver platter. I can't supply you with happiness and neither can your government. It's not our job to make sure every American is happy. Snapping your fingers will not beckon happiness to your soul. Sure, I guess it would be great if every single one of us were content and happy. The crime rate would be down and the production rate would be up. Unfortunately, happiness is elusive to many who are too lazy to pursue it. I've heard so many excuses from friends and acquaintances about why they can't reach their goals for happiness. If they were to put that energy to work, they'd have attained their goals long ago. Many of us realize the opportunities afforded us by our constitution and by our democratic way of life. Others haven't realized that the responsibility for their happiness lies entirely on their shoulders. Could this be because our government has spoiled them? Could it be that their inability to strive to meet goals that would ensure their happiness is due to government assistance? With all of the opportunity available to us why wouldn't we all work to attain happiness?

Our government has opted to take the role of personal responsibility away from us. This is the reason not every single American strives to be as successful or as happy as possible. Why buy the cow when you can get the milk for free, right? Why work to have money if you don't have to buy the cow, and why not just demand a steak when you get hungry?

That's exactly how the American welfare system has conditioned its recipients to think. Is there a legitimate reason for us to expect those dependent on the government to think or behave any other way? Not without retraining them on how to think and change their expectations of entitlement and responsibility. So why then, should we be surprised to hear ridiculous claims that the government, "Owes them?"

A local story I heard a few years ago is typical of the mentality of those "Thirty- somethings" reliant on government assistance. A thirty-four year old lifetime welfare recipient who's been in and out of the county jail for numerous infractions, was finally sent to prison for probation violations. He was quoted saying, "The government should have bought me a damn T.V. and then I wouldn't have been out getting into trouble." I love it because some of the more liberal intellectuals in our society actually sympathize with folks like this. They also agree with the logic that if the government would provide more to keep its low-income citizens happy, there would be less crime and less discontent. Are we to believe that by buying Joe Criminal a television set his tendency to break the law would have been quelled? Could his crime of assault two years ago have been avoided if the government would have only bought him a car? After all, carjacking wouldn't have been "Necessary" if a car had been provided for him. Right? Following that logic, any burglar or thief in prison is being falsely imprisoned or at least wrongly accused of their crime. If the government had provided them with whatever it was they broke the law to obtain, they wouldn't be in the position they are in. Shame on us for being so inconsiderate and stingy. How could we be so insensitive to the needs of potential criminals that we don't intercede with entitlement "Gifts of happiness" before they break the law.

For those able but unwilling to work to obtain happiness, it is expected that someone else will, or should, provide it. Anything received for free has no value, especially if those receiving it are expectant, able and unwilling to work for it. Entitlement leads to abuse and ever-growing expectations of what the government should provide for recipients. Where should we draw the line on happiness entitlements? What if a person tells the government that a Mercedes would make them happy? How do we know that they're not lying and that a Ford Taurus would make them just as happy? The government would have spent thirty thousand more than it had to in order to ensure that citizen's happiness. Abuse, abuse, abuse! What if a twenty-seven inch TV just isn't big enough to bring true happiness to a couch potato? Is the government authorized to spend additional federal dollars on a 52-inch big screen to ensure that individual's happiness? I don't see why not, do you? Maybe we could provide booze to alcoholics who would be unhappy without a buzz and heroine to druggies who would be unhappy without a high. In fact, there should be no reason why we should limit happiness entitlements to one item per recipient. Maybe we could mix it up a little and provide a couch potato/heroine addict/car enthusiast with a big screen TV, a bag of dope and a Ford Taurus to ensure his total and complete happiness. This is great, now he won't have to work to buy a TV and he won't have to steal to afford dope and now he has a car with which he can transport both.

To Liberals, this isn't entitlement....this is enlightenment. When we all realize that buying everybody their happiness is necessary to society's well-being, we will be a much more civilized nation.

Of course it's not the responsibility of America's government to ensure happiness to each and every one of its citizens. Unfortunately, the government has taken so much responsibility for the well-being of its dependents that some actually expect the government to provide any and all things they deem necessary to live a comfortable life. This is entirely the fault of the government. They have helped the low-income and the elderly to some extent, but in the process they have enslaved many who otherwise might be proud, independent Americans. Training and conditioning these folks to depend on government for their quality of life has exposed us to the sad truth of what a "Social experiment gone wrong" looks like.

Instead of expanding benefits and further enabling its dependents, it's time the government reign in the benefits that are taken advantage of by folks who could be, and should be, making their own way in life. This would save taxpayers countless millions of dollars each year and would ensure quality benefits to our elderly and infirm. The truly needy will always be looked after in our country, but now it's time to drop the dead weight bogging the welfare system down. After all, it's not Uncle Sam's job to make us happy. It's true that these folks would be the opposite of happy upon learning that the gravy train was at the end of its tracks. After years of big brother coddling them they would be downright mad that they were being asked to get up and get out and work to support themselves. How could they possibly be expected to supply their own income, food, shelter and happiness?

Unfortunately, after years of reliance on others, many folks would be unable to assimilate and adapt to life in the real world. A generation or two or three with no drive (or real need) to go to college has left the children of lower and middle-income folks largely uneducated and unskilled. A government that doesn't require its citizens to work has guaranteed a lack of work ethic so employers would have no desire to hire these folks. With no concept of dignity, pride or humility, these kids don't have an ice cubes chance in hell to stand on their own and provide for themselves. Therefore, our government chooses to continue to promote the cycle of poverty that has led us to where we are today. I can only imagine what our society will look like in another fifty years.

Already, wealth redistribution and social programs intended to make all citizens equal, are threatening to morph our country into a socialistic society. There is a huge difference between social programs and Socialism. Our government needs to differentiate the two and implement the former with common sense so the latter doesn't envelop our successful capitalistic society.

This means self-sufficiency should once again be considered the norm instead of the exception to the rule. This means happiness should be the responsibility of those seeking it and dignity and pride would once again govern our choices and destinies. It should not be too much to ask for us all to be responsible for our own lives, while at the same time to be willing to assist those physically or mentally unable to do for themselves. It's time we all pull our own weight and quit relying on others to pick up our slack. My wife has a twist on the old saying, "Cart before the horse." In ultra-liberal Oregon she made the observation that, "Pretty soon there will be so many folks in the welfare wagon that there won't be anyone left outside to pull it." How can society function if those who provide the structure become dependents instead of contributors? How long will it be before we completely cannibalize ourselves?

Americans are truly the luckiest people on earth. The opportunities afforded to us by our way of life are as endless as the stars in the sky. Still, Americans must be re-taught that they are in charge of their own destiny. With endless opportunity, we are hampered only by our willingness to work for what it is we want. To truly obtain the goals most of us want for ourselves we need to taste humility, struggle to persevere, give compassion, pursue education and be willing to do for others instead of relying on others to do for us. Initiative and work ethic are as important to success as oxygen and water are to life. With the government providing things that these traits will eventually supply to those who work to master them, Americans simply wont progress as a productive and independent nation. At some point, nobody will be able to obtain happiness. Remember, a person's success is a direct result of ones willingness to achieve.

# CHAPTER 3
# POLITICAL CORRECTNESS

---

One of the biggest threats to our country is political correctness. It undermines our values and our way of life. Each day we hear more stories of how political correctness-gone-wild has usurped more of the American way of life. What began as a social "Nicety" has morphed into an absurd avoidance of truth and the promotion of downright lies concerning morals, history, culture, religion, ethics, policy and righteousness.

Defined by the Canadian Oxford Dictionary, political correctness is: "The avoidance of forms of expression or action that exclude, marginalize, or insult certain racial or cultural groups." It seems that it has also been expanded to include homosexuals, criminals, etc. Basically, any group that differentiates due to culture, religion, or behavior.

So concerned are we, that the truth takes a back seat to the politically correct tiptoeing around "Controversial" topics. These "Controversial" topics are controversial only as a direct result of Americans being politically correct. When in our history, prior to the early 1980's, did an American have to question himself about how to refer to a "Black" person, a "White" person, a "Mexican" person, or an "Indian?" We didn't! We called an "*African American*" Black. We called a "*Native American*" an Indian. We called a "*Hispanic American*" Mexican, and we referred to "*Anglo Saxon Americans*" as White. We were all okay with that and nobody felt offended or put out by being called what we were. It wasn't until our politically correct civil rights extremists deemed it necessary to re-title us all that things began to get confusing. Now, instead of stating the obvious or referring to individuals as anybody with common sense would, we stutter, hesitate, ponder and then hesitantly, in a round-about way, convey what we were trying to say, but couldn't at the risk of possibly offending someone. Sound confusing? It is!

It's not that we're rude. In fact what is now considered "Rude" is only considered so because we've been conditioned, through political correctness, to be ultra-sensitive to the most mundane of things. As a PC nation we no longer refer to things as they are. We refer to things the way the PC crowd wants to envision them. If this means twisting the facts to fit the image, then so be it. Take for example the way we carefully describe an event to say...a police officer. We'll use a traffic accident as an example. The PC explanation: " Officer, I was stopped at this traffic light when suddenly I was hit from behind by this Hispanic-American gentleman driving a slightly less than road worthy vehicle." The way we used to say it? "Sir, I was stopped here when this Mexican guy rear-ended me driving this piece of crap that shouldn't even be on the road."

I had a teacher tell me the following regarding one of the classes my son was having trouble in last year. She told me, "Your son is bright and thoughtful and usually good in class. I think in this case he's just having difficulty applying himself and is easily distracted because he has a hard time grasping the concept we're learning right now."

In return I asked her if my son was doing the work. She said, "No." I asked if he was paying attention in class during the lessons. She said, "He sometimes drifts off." I asked if he was being lazy. She said, "He could apply himself a bit more." "So basically," I said, " He's screwing off in class, he's not paying attention and he's become lazy about his work." "Well, yes," she hesitantly said. I said, "Then why didn't you just say so? I'll deal with my boy and he'll be back on track tomorrow." She then told me that as a teacher she had to be very careful how she worded things while dealing with parents. She said that parents often become offended and defensive when she tells them exactly what their kids are doing in class and what needs to be done to correct the problem. Personally I appreciate a person who just says it like it is. If she would have said, "Your boy is screwing up his grade by goofing off and not doing his work," we could have turned a 30 minute "Conference" into a five-minute meeting. Just say it like it is.

Political correctness leads to all kinds of misunderstanding and wasted time. By not saying what you're trying to say and by re-wording your statements or intentions, the point often gets lost in the translation. So why do we play this PC game? Because we've got a bunch of spineless Liberals, who are so afraid of offending somebody, that they word everything they say in such an amorphous way that not only is nobody offended, nobody understands what the hell it is they just said.

What else has the PC crowd done for us? Well, when was the last time we were hesitant about displaying a manger scene in our front yard due to the possibility of offending someone from Iran, or being sued by a homeowners association or the ACLU? Christmas is under attack because a small group of idiots are worried that the basic religious ideas that our nation was founded on, may offend somebody in America, legally or illegally. Too damn bad if they're offended. It's there prerogative to be offended but it's not my fault that the mention of Jesus or the idea of Santa Claus puts them off. This is America. If an immigrant wants to live here then they better adapt to, or at very least accept, our culture and traditions. The PC crowd seems to ignore the fact that if I, as an American, moved to Afghanistan and was offended by the mention of Allah or The Koran, Afghanistan would not simply abolish their religion so as not to offend me. As a matter of fact, I might actually be persecuted, singled out or even harmed by voicing my offense to their religious traditions. America doesn't kill those who don't follow Judeo-Christian beliefs, but we should expect, at very least, to be able to follow them ourselves. After all, where is it written that I have to conceal or alter my beliefs to accommodate the likes or dislikes of another? Freedom *of* religion, not freedom *from* religion, right?

Want more? It's now politically correct to allow our teenage daughters to obtain abortions without parental notification while at the same time their school is required to get parental permission to give them an aspirin in the nurse's office? Apparently it's politically correct to "Give our pregnant teens privacy" on all matters dealing with the abortion of a fetus, but serious regulations must be followed when dealing with the administration of aspirin on American's campuses. More results of social experiments gone wild. Teens need to be told in no uncertain terms, to place the aspirin between their knees and hold it there until they're married. But wait, that might offend our teens and we certainly can't have that.

Political correctness dictates that you and I should be "Tolerant" to lifestyles that we find morally wrong. "Tolerance" is preached, socially conditioned and now taught to our children in public schools. Tolerance is the PC way of integrating homosexuals, sexual predators, social deviants, criminals and all other genre of misfits and wackos, seamlessly into our society. We are told that being tolerant of others with "Alternate" beliefs and customs is what polite and advanced individuals do. It would be downright impolite to point out any differences between heterosexual and homosexual lifestyles. It would be rude to attempt to keep a "Recovering" sex offender from moving into your neighborhood. Why would anybody possibly be hesitant to trust or fully believe a felon out of prison on parole? It's just not politically correct to do these things or even to discuss them openly.

Political correctness is an intentional lack of directness. The PC folks just can't come out and say *anything*. Instead of saying exactly what they mean or telling us exactly what they think, they shroud their ideas or beliefs in a hazy, fuzzy little cocoon of fluffy talk. An example: Never do they say, "Hey, I've got a better way of doing that." No, they gently say, "Once I saw a guy do that a different way." So what! What is it you're saying? Do you want me to ask you how that other guy did it? I refuse to play the PC game so I say, "Okay." This really bugs them because I didn't play along. They either think I'm really ignorant or that I'm taunting them. It's always fun to watch them squirm and attempt to say the same thing in a different way. The next thing from their mouth is something like, "Yea, he didn't do it like you're doing it." "Yea, I caught that," I say. Then they look at me like…Well, aren't you going to ask me how he did it? No I'm not. If you want me to do it a different way, tell me so, and explain how you'd prefer it done. Simple. To the point.

The PC crowd is offended on a bigger scale any time the United Stated inserts itself into international events. They can't understand why we'd risk offending Middle-Eastern nations by going to war in Iraq.

They are furious that we might piss of Iran if we delve into their Nuclear weapons intentions. North Korea has already been offended by our rude requests to quell their nuclear program. It's no wonder that the PC crowds are the same folks we call Liberals and blend in with the "Blame America" folks who claim to be patriotic while badmouthing the country.

We've seen how ridiculous it has gotten when the PC's start referring to terrorists as "Insurgents", illegal aliens as "Undocumented Americans" and refer to brutal dictators as "Misunderstood leaders." If we say it like it is, we see the truth that terrorists are ruthless murderers, that illegal aliens are threatening the sovereignty of our nation, and that brutal dictators are not misunderstood, just oppressive and brutal.

It's hard not to confuse what is factual from what has been socially conditioned into us when it comes to day-to-day life. For thirty years the PC crowd has gained a foothold in our nation, slowly turning truth to fiction and the obvious into the debated. We've been taught not to offend. Therefore, we don't stand up to them when they try to persuade us to be a more "Gentile and compassionate" nation. The main goal of the PC crowd is to alter reality if reality might offend anyone. They have successfully pulled the wool over our eyes by convincing hundreds of different nationalities, races, groups and individuals, that they *should* be offended. They've convinced Blacks that they are not Black, but "African-Americans" and now they are offended if referred to as Black. They've convinced illegal aliens to infiltrate America by deeming them "Undocumented-Americans" and offering them services intended for American citizens. They've created hate toward America by it's own citizens by calling a justifiable and pre-emptive war in Iraq an "Illegal assault on another nation in the name of oil." They've taken the idea of differences and oddities and developed the concepts of tolerance and diversity.

As a renegade to the whole concept of political correctness, I refuse to follow the PC rules. I am intentionally direct and say things without the fuzzy filter of feel good speech. I am polite in my manner of speech and adhere to common courtesy when engaged in conversation, but I intentionally avoid political correctness. Even so, I sometimes catch myself reverting back to certain niceties as a result of the years of PC conditioning pounded into my head. I'm admittedly a 1993 graduate of the California college system and as so, I've probably received more PC instruction and influence than those who attended college in more conservative states. Students currently attending college are unknowingly drowning in PC curriculum. The instructors are masters of political correctness who strive to instill as much liberal bias into their students as possible. All one needs to do is look at the headlines regarding our nations collegiate stories.

Socialists like Ward Churchill are teaching our children in Colorado how to hate America, capitalism and everything our nation stands for. This "Educator" compares Bush to Hitler and would have us believe that the attack on 9/11 was our fault and that we deserved to have our headquarters of capitalism ruthlessly annihilated. He openly preaches hate toward America. His anger towards our society is blatant.

He confuses capitalism with imperialism and yet he's allowed to instruct and influence our youth. It's politically correct to allow this wing-nut to speak in public forums and it is expected that he be treated with respect and dignity. It doesn't seem to matter anymore that what he preaches should considered treason and what he should be, is hanged. Not likely! In fact Mr. Churchill is regarded with more politeness in most cases than is our president who spends each and every day trying to better our country and defend our nation. Seem kind of backward to anybody?

While Mr. Churchill bashes on ideas and individuals, he's not to be questioned, harassed, or boycotted. To do so would just show how intolerant we are. Thank goodness we've all been trained to be politically correct. It seems, then, that folks like Ann Coulter would also receive the respect and courtesy afforded to an admitted America hater. Coulter, an America lover, is frequently greeted on our nations campuses with protests, boycotts and the occasional physical assault with a cream pie. She is received this way even though she has the courage and intelligence to call a traitor a traitor, a socialist a socialist and an unpatriotic bastard an unpatriotic bastard. I wonder why certain folks are regarded with the highest politically correct standards and others seem not to be covered by PC protection. Could it be that the tolerance Liberals preach is only extended to the ideas and individuals that Liberals wish to tolerate? I do believe that is very hypocritical, don't you?

The PC rules seem to apply to all who have negative outlooks on our nation, our government, our history and our morality. Yet no PC coverage seems to be extended to those who challenge or who denounce America as imperialistic and evil. Unfortunately, in these politically correct times, things seem to have been turned around 180 degrees from sensible. It seems that only in an episode of the Twilight Zone should those who are blatantly unpatriotic be treated with respect and tolerance while those who show patriotism be badmouthed and looked poorly upon. Dee-dee-dee-dee....Dee dee dee dee. Somehow we have arrived smack dab in the middle of the Twilight Zone and are expected to accept these twisted behaviors as the norm.

The selective censorship and social engineering known as political correctness, has been so interwoven into our society that I doubt it can ever be completely erased. It doesn't sound right, it doesn't feel right and it simply shouldn't be tolerated, but after decades of social saturation, political correctness is here to stay. It will remain alive and well because PC rules dictate that we tolerate the educators who teach political correctness to our grade school, high school and college students around the nation.

Inclusivity relates only to those things that the Left wants included in their view of a utopian society. In their distorted view, to exclude things like religion, morality, truthfulness and ethics from our society is not wrong; it's simply their idea of common sense. We've all allowed ourselves to be slowly, but steadily persuaded to accept these concepts as "The way things are," when in fact, the reality that you and I perceive is a totally foreign concept to these intellectual nincompoops.

Why then, do they succeed in undermining *our* common sense? It's simple. We've all been so conditioned to think that offending someone is a "Bad thing," that we just go along with it and never stand up to these mental midgets. We simply don't call them on the carpet on issues regarding political correctness. They taught us the rules of their game before we had a chance to realize the game was being played. Now, to break the rules is simply not acceptable. They've very successfully conditioned us to follow blindly when it comes to being politically correct.

Now we're reaping the results of a country gone super-sensitive. We see the ACLU go bananas every time they think they have a case against anybody who did or said or displayed something that could possibly offend someone else. Political correctness is the reason our country is having the asinine debate over crosses and manger scenes every Christmas. It's also the reason why Halloween celebrations are being banned at elementary schools at an alarming rate. It's why Christianity is being banned from public while minority religions are being celebrated and even promoted.

On a far more important note, political correctness is the reason why it's almost certain that our country will be the target of another successful terrorist attack in the very near future. The folks who demand that the government provide Americans with 100% fail-safe security, are the same people who limit the legitimate and legal avenues with which our government gathers intelligence. Because the idea of a phone tap or FBI surveillance offends these people, they lobby to ban the use of intelligence gathering. No phone taps because the terrorist calling from Algeria would not know the CIA was listening in on him and then might incriminate himself or reveal his plans to bomb Chicago....and that's just not fair. No police tailing of suspects because the suspect doesn't know he's being followed. He might purchase some explosives or do something else illegal to assist terrorists while being watched....and that's just not fair. We certainly don't want to profile folks. Just because a Middle-Eastern man between 18 and 45 years of age boards a plane wearing a trench coat with a metal barrel sticking out the bottom of it, doesn't mean we should assume he might hijack that plane. If he were singled out and prevented from killing innocent people on that plane as a result of profiling, that would probably offend him....and that's just not fair.

We've been handcuffed and asked to fight a war on terror. We've been hog-tied and told to defend ourselves. We've been stripped of our intelligence gathering abilities and told to predict terrorist attacks. We've been denied the use of our common sense and told to use reason to identify possible terrorists. As I said before, political correctness turns common sense around 180 degrees and expects you to go along with "The way things are." Even issues as dire and serious as our national security and way of life are not exempt from the PC game. When the PC's win, America and patriotic Americans lose. It's the inevitable and desirable outcome of a game designed and engineered by traitorous and subversive Liberals who hate America. The longer we all play, the more likely they are to win the game.

# CHAPTER 4

# DEMOCRACY VERSUS DEMOCRATS

Our country would not be the strong and successful country it is today if we turned control of the United States of America over to the Democrat Party. In fact it wouldn't even vaguely resemble the America we know and love. It's a simple fact that their ultimate goal is socialism and therefore they cannot be trusted.

The American Heritage Dictionary defines democracy as: 1) "A government by the people, exercised either directly or through elected representatives." 2) "Social and political equality and respect for the individual within the community." Since modern-day Democrats advocate neither for a government of the people and give little respect to individuals in any community, they really can't be considered "Democrats" according to the above definition.

Let's look at what the same source defines as socialism. "A system or theory of social organization in which the producers possess both political power and production and distribution means." In other words, socialists want to control what you possess and how you live and will distribute to you what they feel you need. Does this remind you of any number of our "Democrat" leaders who are forever fighting for control of our healthcare, our food assistance programs, our housing assistance programs, etc.? They want to control how we live. Period. Referred to as "Liberals" here in America, these socialists-in-disguise, favor the use of public resources to promote what they refer to as "Social progress." This "Social progress" includes the indoctrination of our school age children into the acceptance of the homosexual lifestyle, the persecution of Christian beliefs and ridiculously bloated social assistance programs. They represent all that America isn't.

Would you trust the security of America to modern-day Democrats? Would you trust the well-being of your children to the modern-day Democrats? Do today's Democrats present themselves as strong on any issue that is important to preserving our way of life? Why do Democrats strive to undermine our leadership every chance they get? How did Democrats shed their moral backbone and become ethical jellyfish? How do Democrats expect intelligent Americans to support their policies or back their "Leadership?" Leadership supplied by modern day Democrats cannot sustain our democracy. Their stance on National Defense alone should be enough to convince anybody with a shred of sense that they are inept to stand up to those wishing to harm us. Their defense of terrorist's rights and the scrutiny of prisoner's treatment over the safety and morale of our troops is reprehensible. Their desire to appease the enemy in order to avoid conflict and to compromise our national security to sidestep military implementation is irresponsible and dangerous.

Democrats are sick and tired of democracy. Democracy is impeding their goal of transitioning our country into a socialist utopia. Why even call Democrats, Democrats? These days, except for an infinitesimal few, the Democrat Party is nothing more than liberal extremists. Those who still hold on to the title of Democrat cringe when their "Fellow" leftists publicly reveal their beliefs and goals.

These Liberals have no backbone. It is for no other reason that our country is vulnerable to terrorist attack and is obscenely fiscally irresponsible. As democrats on socialist steroids, Liberals are doing their best to bring down the financial system that allows our country to remain atop the financial world. Instead of recruiting suicide bombers to fly jets into our financial headquarters, Liberals tax and fine and punish our nation's successful moneymaking companies to the point of breaking. The philosophy is to punish anybody who makes more money than liberals think they should have. Therefore, individuals or corporations who have risen to the top of the financial world through hard work, experience, education and determination, are to be punished and stripped of their wealth. Redistribution cannot be achieved if there are so many classes of people. Rich folks have too much money, poor folks have too little money and middle-class folks could do with a little less to insure everybody has the same amount.

Liberals will tell you this is fair and makes sense. While I'm sure some of the very poorest in our society might be convinced of this (as it would increase their personal wealth through no responsibility of their own) I can assure you that nobody else working to persevere and succeed thinks it sounds too good.

On so many levels our modern day Democrats are actively working to undermine the very democracy that allows them power and privilege. Instead of being elected to positions of power, they'd prefer to appoint one another into leadership roles and forego the whole election process altogether. As insane as it sounds, Liberals don't want common Americans to have individual rights. Liberals feel they are superior to the rest of us and therefore have no faith in our ability to make educated decision regarding important topics such as their ability to lead. In other words, Democrats despise true democracy. It stifles their plans of elitism and is a hurdle to shaping a more socialistic society.

When the Democrat Party is lead by the likes of Ted Kennedy, Dick Durbin, Dr. Howard Dean and John Kerry, America has a problem. When Mrs. Clinton, Dianne Feinstein and Barbara Boxer openly reveal their distain for common Americans and denounce the rights assured to us all, we need to worry. These are the figureheads threatening the American way of life. These "Leaders" and many others, are pushing to mitigate the importance of our constitutional rights. They cloud the intentions of our founding fathers by re-writing history and twisting facts to fit their figures. They are only out for themselves and their agenda. There is precious little room for you or I to get in their way with our trivial ideas, traditions or concerns. These people simply can't be trusted with the fate of our nation.

If we were to trust Dianne Feinstein we would no longer be allowed to own personal firearms. It wasn't too long ago that as Mayor of San Francisco, she made it apparent that she felt only military and law enforcement personnel were deemed worthy of possessing firearms. Oh yea, she herself felt the need to carry a concealed weapon and was caught red handed being a hypocrite. Apparently her life and safety is more important than the lives and safety of those who elected her. Thanks largely in part to her early efforts, residents of San Francisco are now banned from owning handguns in the city limits. In fact as of January 1, 2006 gun owners in San Fran had 90 days to turn over their firearms to law enforcement. If they don't? Well all guns sold in California are registered to the owner so we can only assume that quiet confiscations will begin and houses will be entered by law enforcement to physically "Repossess" these weapons. And she claims to be a proponent for individual's rights? Mrs. Feinstein's utopia looks like it's beginning to take shape in California's liberal epicenter. Imagine our entire nation entrusting our second amendment right to Mrs. Feinstein. Scary thought, eh?

Let's imagine we entrust our freedom of speech to Howard Dean. Mr. Dean has stated that he, "Hates Republicans." He has stated that republicans are idiots and should not be listened to. With a true talent for schoolyard name calling Doctor Dean has made it clear that anyone who has opinions or beliefs that differ from his own, need not speak. These "stupid" people obviously have nothing to contribute to our society through suggestions or ideas and therefore are basically useless. Howard Dean doesn't want to be an elected leader, he wants to rule over you while stifling your opinions and silencing your voice. Let's look at some of the morality he lends his voice of support to, according to the New York Times. Mr. Dean worked hard to pass Vermont's civil union legislation that grants basic legal rights to same-sex couples. He supports same sex immigration (H.R.832), which allows US citizens to sponsor same-sex partners for immigration into America. He supports abolishing the "Don't ask, don't tell" policy so that homosexuals can serve openly (and therefore flamboyantly) in our armed forces. He's big on gay and lesbian adoption too. It sounds to me like he should be in charge of the People's Republic of San Francisco instead of the Democrat Party. Do we still want to trust leadership of any kind to the demented Doctor?

Let's take a look at our national security in the hands of G.I. John Kerry. A Vietnam vet and America-bashing hero to the Jane Fonda crowd, he proclaimed himself a strong leader during the 2004 elections. Can our national security be trusted to an individual who demonized the US military following his service? This is a man who has some serious commitment issues as well. He can't commit to one point of view and stick with it. He humors audiences with what he thinks they want to hear and then changes his "Views" as he prepares to address another group at another venue. He's for the war...He's against the war. He voted to approve military spending before he voted to deny it. He's proud of our military men...though he proclaims they raze villages in the fashon of Gangues Kahn. He'll be strong on national defense by cutting military spending to reduce the national debt or enhance social programs.

What are we to believe? What I believe, is that this is a man would sell his own mother to gain more power. He's a man who is as unprincipled as he is unworthy of our trust. If we can't trust his word how can we entrust our security?

How much faith should we trust to a moral compass like Ted Kennedy? A man born into wealth and treated with the privilege usually reserved for royalty, Ted still couldn't mind his P's and Q's (literally) and has filled the role of black sheep in a well-to-do family. A living legacy to a family of tragedy, Ted has worked hard to keep scandal and shame at the forefront of the Kennedy name since the late 1960's. An ethical man, who killed his mistress while driving drunk late at night in the now infamous town of Chappaquiddick, Ted has served his constituents in Massachusetts "Faithfully" for decades. Although once expelled from Harvard for cheating on a Spanish exam, he walks with the air of all other elites who feel they are superior to, and far brighter than you and I. Old Ted has cast votes for nearly every law that limits individual rights (except for the rights of homosexuals) and opposes the idea of democracy. He supports gays and opposes gun ownership. He's also been a huge supporter of government assistance programs. According to Ted, there's never enough money to justify the national defense budget but there's always plenty of money for welfare and dozens of other social programs...

Especially if those bills are filled with pork bellies and kickbacks. Ted's a true conundrum to reason and an embarrassment to Democracy. In other words, he's a strong and respected leader among Democrats. Should we trust our nation to his higher morals and uncompromising defense of our nation's working class?

And then there's Hillary. What can we say about Hillary that she hasn't already said about herself? Only the truth! She's a woman among women showing all good and decent gals around the nation how to gracefully deal with the multiple marital infidelities of a chauvinistic husband (especially if you stand to lose status and money by blowing the whistle on your hubby). She stands strong for whatever she feels strongly about in front of a given crowd. She's pro-choice in the presence of the National Organization of Women and she doesn't necessarily favor abortion when surrounded by a more conservative crowd. She sticks to her guns when condemning the president for going to war in Iraq but she supports our military efforts there. As the first lady, Mrs. Clinton supported universal healthcare, gun bans, social programs and huge government spending initiatives. As New York senator, with aspirations of running for President, she scurries to the political middle in a feeble attempt to hide her true liberal intentions. She's a real wolf in sheep's clothing. She's truly as honest in her deception as she is deceptive in her honesty. I say, "We've already had a Clinton for president and she didn't do too well the first time around."

What all of these "Liberal leaders" have in common is a distain for America and a low tolerance for the traditional beliefs that created an unwavering nation. They blatantly spit in the face of common sense related to national security, morality, ethical behavior and the preservation of America.

It's the job of a Liberal to actively work to subvert and undermine the very fabric that makes up

America. As a result, they are often accurately labeled as unpatriotic by the rest of us. They don't like that! Just listen to Hillary's rants when she's referred to as unpatriotic. With the shrillest of voices, and at the top of her liberal lungs, she proclaims her patriotism and denounces anyone who would question her allegiance to our country. What she and other Liberals don't realize is that their actions speak louder than their words and their actions show us that they're anything but patriotic.

Liberals have puffed out their collective chests and proven to us that any attempt America makes to become self sufficient in terms of energy is met with fierce opposition by the environmental left. Any attempt to strengthen our military is met with fierce opposition by the spineless appeasement crowd of the political Left. Our efforts to instill morality in our youth are met with Liberal's accusations of bigotry, intolerance or prejudice. Attempts to better educate our children through sensible programs, such as school vouchers, are rebuffed in an effort to keep their minds dull. Even the ability to express one's faith in Christianity is under attack from these secularist elites. In other words, every effort we make to better our nation is met with opposition by today's political left. How does working against America's well being qualify as patriotism?

Liberals have taken the rights granted to all of us by our constitution and used them against America itself in ways our founding fathers would find appalling if not down right traitorous. The ACLU is the biggest violator of common sense and hides behind numerous constitutional rights to defend wrongdoers nation-wide. Civil liberties come with civil responsibilities. Without displaying the latter, the former can hardly be expected. Yet somehow our liberal figureheads twist facts and distort truth in a pathetic effort to convince us that the idea of "Right" is not concrete, and that "Wrong" is subjective. How else could they excuse their own behavior as well as the actions of murderers, rapists and other felons they defend?

There you have it. These are the leaders of the modern Democrat Party. It's a party that would like nothing more than to do away with the idea of Democracy here in America. Socialism is their goal and whatever means it takes to achieve their goal is viewed as a necessary evil. Individual rights, religious rights, morality, ethics, and family values are all things that can be compromised and sacrificed in the eyes of Liberals if it means finally establishing their new Utopia. They're as transparent as they are unrealistic. They're shameless and seemingly proud of their scandals and questionable behavior. They exaggerate and lie much like you and I work to pay bills, and they have no qualms about lying to us *about* their lies. For some unknown reason they expect you and I to follow them blindly because they tell us how smart and superior they are. I don't buy it and so far neither do the majority of good Americans. As long as we don't get so wrapped up in their smooth talk that we can't see the forest for the trees, we'll continue to have the upper hand on these arrogant elitist asses. So say it like it is the next time you hear of a liberal doing something else to undermine America.

## Chapter 5
# The Flawed Food Stamp System

Oh how far we've come and how compassionate we are. Bureaucrats have invited folks to dinner. Millions of Americans eat at the government table each and every month. And each and every month we hear that kids are going hungry and low-income families are suffering because there's not enough food to feed them all. Government funds that pay for food stamps, (as well as dozens of other entitlement programs) come from Washington D.C. They are collected and allocated each year in a feeble and ill-guided effort to end hunger in the United States. As a huge band-aid, food stamps do nothing more than serve the "Give a man a fish" mentality. We're called insensitive and heartless if we demand these people eventually feed themselves by "Learning to fish." To stay in the good graces of many different groups, organizations, and voters, politicians have yet to address the abuses, problems and waste associated with our bloated food stamp system. In fact, there are advocates actively recruiting individuals to use food stamps (due to a surplus of funds) for the sake of insuring the food stamp budget increase during the next funding cycle. After all, if there's money left at the end of the year, maybe the program doesn't require so much funding. Since social program funds are seldom reduced, and never cut, it stands to reason that promoting usage of food stamps among those who might not otherwise "Take advantage" of them, is a logical tactic.

In fact, those who lobby for ever increasing federal dollars to provide ever increasing amounts of food and services for "The poor," are doing nothing more than inflating numbers and crying wolf regarding the degree of need here in the "Land of plenty." By increasing numbers to simply increase funding they refuse to see that their actions are only hurting those who truly and legitimately depend on assistance to get by. Spreading services thin to the seniors and disabled by offering assistance to low-income individuals fully capable (if unwilling) to support themselves, takes food out of the mouths of individuals that the program was originally designed to help. These activists, lobbyists, and advocates use scare tactics and guilt trips to shame you and I into believing our fellow citizens are living like the truly needy in some distant third world country. They promote gloom and doom to obtain funding increases while at the same time quieting anyone who might question the legitimacy of "Feeding the poor." The media sensationalizes these stories and claims to take an "Objective look at poverty in America." At this point, anybody who would stand up and say, "Let's work to reduce the billions we're spending on food stamps," would inevitably be viewed as a ruthless uncaring ogre who wants nothing more than to hurt America's most vulnerable, low-income citizens.

What we sometimes overlook is the fact that for the government to increase funding to these programs each year, they have to get that money from somewhere. In fiscal year 2003 the total federal food stamp costs were $23.88 billion dollars. That's billion, with a "B." As more funds are allotted and more individuals are convinced to "Take advantage" of the food stamp program, the taxes paid by working Americans will continue to increase. Let's not forget that the Federal Government has no money. It creates revenue by taking money from you and I as we earn it. By working to support ourselves, we are inadvertently paying to support those who cannot or will not support themselves. Few of us have a problem lending a helping hand to those physically or mentally unable to feed themselves. Forking over my hard-earned cash to buy groceries for those able but unwilling to buy their own groceries, is another story altogether. For the most part, as a citizen of this country, I am unable to choose where my tax dollars go. We are forced to trust our politicians to use our tax dollars to best benefit of the country. That's a lot like putting the fox in charge of the henhouse. I personally support the use of tax dollars on national defense and most funding dealing with infrastructure. Drastically cutting the fat of social programs would allow every working American to keep more of their hard earned money. It would also yank the very comfortable rug out from under the feet of those abusing the system, and would force them to support themselves. It's a fact that as a country's government grows, so does the burden of increasing taxes. The taxes are used to pay for the increase in size. Where will the line be drawn and when will we require more personal responsibility of the poor and demand fewer taxes be paid by the rest of us?

Where once the private sector provided assistance, compassion and support for the needy in our cities and towns, it is now the government that runs the poverty management business. What was once an efficient and practically cost-free system of looking out for our family, friends and neighbors, is now a multi-billion dollar social machine that engulfs and absorbs everything it touches. Once it was a person's goal to be self-reliant and any dependency on others reflected poorly on that individual's ability to be self-sufficient. Accepting a hand out in tough times was a humbling, humiliating, and usually short-term experience. With the government in charge of handouts, dignity, self worth and short-term assistance are words of a bygone day. Over the past several decades the politically correct crowd has somehow convinced Americans that entitlement is dignified and handouts, while expected, are never to be appreciated. The concepts of pride, dignity and humility have no meaning for those who rely on the government for their food, housing, medical coverage and more.

Let me clarify that the comments in this chapter refer to those receiving food stamps who are able bodied individuals and able, but unwilling to support themselves. I've stated before, and will reiterate here, that as a compassionate society, few of us have a problem with assisting those who are elderly, handicapped, mentally impaired, or otherwise truly unable to support themselves.

What really irritates me, and the reason the food stamp system is not nearly efficient as it should be, are those who find a way to take advantage of a system designed to help the truly needy. I don't believe that a person who is able to work is truly needy simply because he refuses to work. Laziness and complacency have been rewarded and the abuse rate in the food stamp arena (as well as the far less regulated food bank system) has risen steadily over the years. This does nothing but reduce the quality of help available to our nations elderly and infirm. Thus, I believe my dander and animosity toward those described in this chapter is justifiable as well as understandable.

As a thirty something myself, I'm sorry to say that I'm largely ashamed of my own generation. In my day-to-day routine I can see where work ethic, drive, personal goals, and pride in a job well done are largely lacking in those who range in age from 20 – 35, and often older. I truly believe that those born in the late 60's and early 70's were the last to receive from their parents the instruction and moral fortitude that had made Americans strong and independent in the generations that preceded them.

By watching their parents work hard and strive to better their well being, children learned those very same traits. Taking pride in the ownership of an item you worked hard to earn is the true reward of ownership. Likewise, children raised in a household where their parents have no daily routine, no job and no drive grow to emulate their mentors. If all one has to do to eat and pay bills is walk to the mailbox on the first of each month to pick up a government check and food stamps, what motivation would one have to find gainful employment? America has successfully bred and raised three to four generations of welfare families. This is a job well done according the political left. By masking dependence as compassion for poor folks, social engineers have transformed healthy, able-bodied individuals into lazy, unmotivated dependants. Current recruitment of the next generation of poor folks is termed by advocates "Food stamp outreach." It's a catch phrase to be wary of.

By making poverty comfortable (in many cases, very comfortable) the government has insured the ongoing poverty of most of those who receive "Assistance."

Comparable to keeping the proverbial wife "Barefoot and pregnant," dependants on welfare are kept at home and reliant on the government to be the family breadwinner. By receiving something for nothing, low-income individuals have no sense of ownership or responsibility for the assistance they receive. Therefore, many recipients use their benefits irresponsibly instead of frugally, like the rest of us who have to work for our income. What's more, the federal government refuses to put common sense restrictions on the items that recipients are able purchase with their "Free" money.

## FOOD STAMP PRODUCTS

I mentioned before that bureaucrats have been inviting too many able bodied folks to dinner. Would it be too much to expect these folks to eat what we put before them? Apparently that idea is not only cruel and insensitive, but I've been told that it may well be an infringement on their freedom of choice. Our society has deteriorated so much since the inception of FDR's "New Deal" that a poor person receiving help to survive through the depression would be appalled to see what today's "Poor person" is buying at the supermarket. Once beans, rice, flour, potatoes, butter, milk, and sugar were staples that food vouchers provided a family. These staple items were used, alongside any other food products a family could obtain, to prepare hearty meals like casseroles, stews and foods that would feed a family for several days. Today's high fat, high calorie and high cost processed foods have created a generation of food stamp recipients who border on obesity and have developed heart disease and diabetes at an alarming rate. Their health is of no concern to them, though, because you and I pay for their healthcare costs, too. More on that later.

Let's take a look at what our tax dollars are buying for those who our bureaucrats have invited to dinner. Actually, let's first take a look at the short list of what food stamps *can't* be used for. According to The Department of Human Services food stamps cannot be used for the following: 1.Non-food items including pet food, paper products, hygiene products and cosmetics. 2.Alcohol or tobacco. 3.Medicines/vitamins 4.Food to be eaten in the store. 5.Hot foods ready to eat including deli and restaurant food. That's it! Everything else is fair game.

Remembering that food stamps were instituted to keep poor folks from starving during difficult times, does it make sense that they can be used in grocery stores to buy boneless skinless chicken breasts, deli meat, T-bone steaks, prawns, veil cutlets, lobster tails and baby-back ribs? Is it a smart thing to waste food stamps on high dollar items like hot pockets, toaster pastries, "Meals-in-a-box", frozen entrees, TV dinners and frozen pizzas when you are trying to feed a hungry family? Also, to keep a poor family from starving, food stamps can be used to purchase soda pop, chips, ice cream, pre-packaged gourmet coffee, pop corn, candy bars and beef jerky.

If that isn't enough to feed a starving family, food stamps can also be used at take-and-bake pizza joints and to buy frozen meats and seafood from gourmet food delivery services.

Apparently eating at my table does not mean you have to eat what I am eating. There are more people who are paying taxes for food stamp recipients to buy these high-end foods than can afford to buy these foods themselves. If that doesn't seem hypocritical of our tax and waste government, then I don't know what does. There's a fundamental problem when those who support social programs cannot afford to live as well as those who are receiving assistance.

So how can we get low-income individuals to use their food stamps more wisely? My suggestion is to require any and all food stamp recipients under the age of 50 to attend a mandatory budgeting class and a series of cooking classes as a stipulation of receiving assistance. Since they never learned from their parents how to shop responsibly and to prepare meals from raw ingredients instead of a box, it's unlikely that they will teach their children the skills needed to feed and support a family. Therefore, another stipulation would be to require the children (school age kids) to attend these classes with their parents. We might as well get a head start on teaching the next generation before it's too late. This idea is largely received with enthusiasm when I discuss it with those who are paying to provide folks with food stamps. The reaction is a bit different when I mention it to those receiving assistance. They tell me that being required to attend a class in order to receive food stamps every month is wrong and illegal. I've been told that if classes were required that they'd just give up the food stamps before being forced to do something to receive them. I ask, "How hungry, really hungry, are these folks if they'd refuse the opportunity to better themselves through a couple of educational and life-skills classes in return for free food every month." I know I sound cruel and insensitive but I'm sure we could greatly reduce the caseload (if not educate it) if we were to simply institute a policy like the one I just described.

So comfortably content are America's poor that the mere suggestion of them doing something in order to receive assistance is not just an inconvenience to them, it's downright offensive. We should all be aware by now that it is their God given right to receive as much public assistance as they can qualify for, while not being required to do anything in return. Where have all of us thickheaded, demanding, insensitive, cold-hearted bastards been for the past thirty years? Oh how far we've come.

I'm reminded of a situation I witnessed two years ago at a local grocery store. While standing in line at the store, I watched the "Gentleman" in front of me loading the conveyor belt with his groceries, including steaks, ice cream, sodas and various other items. Among those items was a 40 pound bag of dog food. When the cashier gave a total, the man pulled from his wallet an Oregon Trail card (Oregon's dignified payment method for low-income residents.) This credit card style piece of plastic could be used to pay for everything on the counter sans the dog food. When the cashier told the man that he couldn't purchase pet food with food stamps he got upset. What he did next nearly earned him a good old-fashioned ass whoopin'. He told the clerk, "Fine. I guess my God damn dogs will just have to eat steak then."

And with that, he proceeded back to the meat counter where he returned with 4 packages of London broil steaks. He dropped the bag of dog food on the ground, shoved the steaks at the clerk and then used his card to pay for his groceries *and* his dog's steaks. If that wasn't enough to baffle the small crowd now standing near the check stand witnessing this situation, he then told the clerk that he had to pay for the beer on the bottom shelf of his cart and that he needed a carton of Camel light cigarettes. Cash was pulled from the same wallet that held his government funded food stamp card. He paid for the beer and smokes and was on his way. Oh, by the way, his cigarettes and case of beer cost him just over forty dollars.

It seems, to this cruel and insensitive observer, that he should have used his cash to purchase his food and not his vices. But why should he? If there are no stipulations stating what you and I see as obvious, and if he has no shame paying for food with food stamps in front of a small crowd and then paying cash for smokes and beer, how are we to expect him to change his habits? Is this the type of individual I want my tax dollars going to "Help?" Is this the type of starving American that the food stamp system was originally designed to help?

There have been a few states that have tossed around the idea of limiting the type of products that food stamps could be used for. Complicating the idea of limiting purchasable products is the fact that the grocery industry makes billions by selling low-nutrition, high-profit convenience foods to food stamp users. The uproar from the grocery industry would be deafening should any movement towards purchasing limitations gain momentum. It's all about money. It's not about personal responsibility, right and wrong or anything else. Morally, grocers might see that low-income people buying high dollar food with free money is wrong, but the quarterly earnings report is bound to snuff out morals.

Some critics of the idea of limiting food stamp usage gripe, "If you hate big government so much, then why put government in charge of what poor people eat?" My reply is that the government chose to take on the role of poverty manager. They stepped in, picked up the poor, and have cradled and pampered them. The least they could do is mange their poverty responsibly.

If they're going to do it, then they should damn well do it right?

The same advocates complain that it would be cruel to regulate the types of food poor people can eat. I'm not trying to regulating what they eat, just what they can buy on my dime. Is that so unreasonable? Are we offering compassion or unconditional coddling?

## POLITICS AND FOOD

By bastardizing compassion and allowing (even promoting) the abuse of the food stamp system, our government has taken away the need for a breadwinner in the house. If you factor in all of the other benefits that low-income folks "Qualify" for, there is really no need for a father figure or man-of-the house at all. Papa government now pays the bills for any and all that need assistance.

While we continue to enslave yet another generation of welfare recipients, the very Democrat Party who claims to be compassionate and representative of the downtrodden and destitute, do nothing more than insure a life of dependence and repression for those they claim to help. These same Democrats bash Republicans and Conservatives claiming that they don't care about the poor and do nothing to provide for the low-income folks here in America. It's all about politics. It's ridiculous to claim that the current administration, which now spends more money on food stamps and numerous other social programs than any other administration in history, does nothing to "Help" the poor. I don't agree with the administration's decision to continually allocate more federal dollars to a program that is utterly corrupt and flawed, but claims that the Right does nothing are simply untrue.

To look through the eyes of a low-income person here in America, we might see the allure of receiving something for nothing. It goes something like this. We'll use me as an example. Lets say that one day while listening to the radio at work, I hear an advertisement for food stamp assistance. Knowing, that as a single parent, my full time job just barely puts food on the table and pays the bills, I call the toll free number and inquire about eligibility. Come to find out, I make a little too much to qualify for substantial benefits. I'm told that if I ask to have my work hours (see income) cut a little bit then I can qualify for a significant amount of food stamps as well as many other social programs that can "Help" me. Working just thirty hours a week now I receive two hundred and fifty dollars a month in food stamps, have a monthly voucher that lowers the amount I'm required to pay for rent, qualify for state paid daycare, enroll in the state provided healthcare and receive a cash benefit for living expenses. Living more comfortably that I did previously, I am now very content to work my part time job and make little enough to continue to receive my monthly benefits. I have no motivation to work harder, to work up the company ladder or to seek education to obtain a higher paying job. The gap between wage and benefits is too great to motivate me to better myself. Hooked! For how long? That is up to the individual receiving benefits, but many in this situation stay comfortably impoverished for years or decades. This is the game and those playing it are politicians who line their social services department's pockets with millions of dollars. The only winners are those who are allocated an ever-increasing amount of funds and the losers are those sucked into dependence. Money makes the world go 'round so it's no wonder there's a push to recruit and produce more poor people.

Political advocates who fight for the "Rights" of poor people cause an even bigger problem than the bureaucrats. There are a few advocates for the poor who genuinely want to help low-income folks get out of poverty. Unfortunately the tactics they use to do so are always counterproductive to their goals. These champions of the downtrodden advocate for increased benefits for those already reliant on government handouts. They scream for more food stamp dollars and increased social service budgets. They demand dignity for the poor and criticize anybody who asks the question that really needs to be answered to begin to solve the problem of poverty. What is that question you might ask? "*Why are these people poor?*"

If advocates for the poor would work toward answering *that* question they would begin to see what real barriers low-income folks face. From there, they could work towards giving these folks what they need to be self sufficient instead of giving them the assistance required to make them dependant. Advocates should want to be put out of business for a lack of need instead of insuring their jobs by creating more need. Unfortunately, the demand for food stamps trumps the demand to get these poor folks educated. Requests for budget increases to social services drown out requests to get poor folks trained in a trade or profession, or at least taught some income-earning skills. Since a good portion of low-income people are in their situation because they're under-educated or unskilled, it would make sense to teach and educate them, wouldn't it?

Nobody ever says to a poor person, "You live the way you do because you dropped out of high school when you got pregnant and never completed your GED. How do you expect to get a job when you compete with people who have college degrees or at least a diploma?" It may be blunt but it's the truth. It's never mentioned because we're required to show respect and dignity to poor folks. Even if that means never addressing the reasons for their poverty. In order to address hunger and begin to find solutions, we need to say it like it is!

The mere fact that food stamps and the accompanying debates, arguments, funding issues and political attention is an issue at all, is somewhat ridiculous. Nowhere in our constitution and nowhere in our bill of rights are citizens of the United States guaranteed the right to be fed. Yet some argue that they have the right to be happy and that being fed is integral to that right. Not so. We are guaranteed the right to *pursue* happiness. It is not the government's job to make us happy. To win the pursuit of happiness and to actually obtain it, one must be fed. It seems, then, that Americans are obligated to feed themselves in order to be happy. What if the government decided to take on the role of "Happiness Insurers" as they have taken the role of Poverty Managers? As we've already discussed, the thought of the government striving to make every American happy is as ridiculous as it would be impossible. Yet they've basically tried do the same thing by creating and expanding the food stamp system and various other social programs.

We've removed all sense of shame and instilled dignity to assistance that was once undignified. We've created generations with a mentality that expect the government to look after them. We're called mean spirited when we question the need for such a huge program. We have made people as dependent on government as they are on the air we breath. We have let out the reigns and will never be able to pull them tight again. How did we create such a mess in such a relatively short time? We gave people something for nothing. That's all it took to turn a country full of proud, self-supporting, hard working individuals into the food stamp recipients we see in our stores today. That's why it amazes me that even after acknowledging assistance of this type often breeds dependence, our government and advocates continue to promote the growth of the food stamp system.

Any time the government gets involved with the mundane aspects of day-to-day life of it's citizens, things are bound to go wrong. This has been the case with social programs since the institution of the 1935 work relief program for the unemployed. Originally a way to address the problems that were generated as the result of the Great Depression, public assistance and social programs have morphed into nearly unrecognizable images of their former selves. In 1961 the food stamp pilot program was launched. Thirteen years later, in 1974 the food stamp program was up and running nation wide. According to Department of human Services numbers in 2002 we were spending more than *forty-one million dollars* a day on food stamps. The 18 billion we spent on food stamps in 2002 grew to 23.88 billion in 2003. That's an increase of nearly 6 billion dollars in one year. Advocates would tell you that if they were promised a seven billion dollar increase and only got six, that the government had cut a billion dollars to food stamp funding. It wasn't cut, it was increased by six billion dollars but that's the way advocates raise their alarmist voices and act appalled that the government would "Cut" funding to the poor.

Food stamps are such big business that over 9 million households and more than twenty million individuals receive food stamp assistance. In 2002 the national average monthly benefit was $79.00 per person and over $185.00 per household. This money flows out of Washington D.C. each and every month and the flow will never slow or stop. The ever-increasing amount of funds channeled into the food stamp program is as inevitable as it is unconscionable.

Doesn't a government who works aggressively to repress and make dependent it's citizens, seem like an example of Soviet or Communist rule? It sure doesn't sound like the way Americans would be treated by their government, does it? But this is how our government has decided to "Take care" of us. When the government controls your food budget they've got your attention, don't they?

## SCHOOL AND SUMMER LUNCHES

More government assistance and millions of additional dollars are wasted every day in our schools during the school year and in our parks during the summer months. They're called free breakfast and lunches, reduced breakfast and lunches and summer lunch programs.

If a child belongs to a family that receives food stamps or TANF (Temporary Assistance for Needy Families), or participates in the Food Distribution Program on Indian Reservations, he or she automatically qualifies for free meals at school. Homeless children, as well as migrant and runaway kids, also get free meals.

In 2003-04 school year there were nearly twenty-nine million kids who participated in the National School Lunch Program. An average school day during that time frame saw sixteen and half million kids receiving free or reduced lunches. A reduced meal means that the student's family can be charged no more than forty cents per meal. The government reimburses some 98,000 schools and care facilities that serve free and reduced meals. A school or agency that served a free lunch in 2003-04 was reimbursed $2.32. For a reduced lunch they were reimbursed $1.92. Likewise free breakfasts were reimbursed $1.23, and $.93 for reduced. Studies showed that an average of 8.7 million kids received free or reduced breakfasts during 03-04.

Now that we know the stats the facts and the figures, we can ask the question. Why?

Are we just *trying* to get young children used to getting things for free? Are we *trying* to make it "Normal" for kids to feel okay about the government taking care of them? I guess it's a good strategy to groom these future dependents, if that's your goal.

Another, "Why." Why are we feeding the children of the folks that we're giving food stamps to? Why do they receive food stamps if not to feed their family? Do these folks not spend their "Free" money wisely on bread and peanut butter and bologna so they can make lunches for their children to take to school? I see this as an obvious duplication of services and the government could eliminate the twin services and save a bundle of money each year.

We know that a hungry child doesn't perform as well in class as a well-nourished child does. Nutrition is essential to a child's education and ability to learn. Therefore, the parents should be doubly concerned about their children getting the nutrition they need before heading off to school. It is the responsibility of the parent, not the government, to make sure kids are fed and taken care of. Why have we taken the responsibility off the parents and placed it squarely on the shoulders of the government and the taxpayers?

I'll tell you why, at the risk of sounding cruel. It's because some parents are incapable or unwilling to take care of their own children. Advocates for the poor constantly remind us that it is not the child's fault that the parent is addicted to drugs, or is too lazy to pack a kid's lunch, or to self-absorbed to pay attention to the child's needs. They expect this argument to garnish support for their programs by dangling poor innocent "Starving" kids in front of us. After all, who'd ever deny a hungry child a meal? By playing the "Emotions" game, advocates are somehow excused from addressing the real issue of why kids are going without. It's simply because the parents are unfit! If ever there was a case for sterilization, these parents are it. Cruel I know, but continuing to coddle the parents only generates another group of dependants...their children.

What you'll never hear from these hunger activists is that the parents take no responsibility for their children because they've never been asked to. For a majority of these parents, the government has picked up the pieces of their lives, and in the process, has taken over the responsibility of raising their children as well. Why work when there is no consequence for not working? Why spend food stamps on staple items if I'm allowed to buy steak and cake? Why get up early to feed my kids when the government will feed them at school for me? Why take the initiative to be a responsible parent when someone else is willing to raise my kids?

All of the touchy feel-good programs initiated to help people have come back to do just the opposite of helping people. These programs ruin lives by creating dependence, breeding apathy, and neutering ones self-worth. All these character-destroying traits are essential to creating a society totally and completely reliant on government assistance. I'm sure that this was not the original intent of assistance programs but the effects of entitlement on society have been studied and noted over the past several decades. Yet we still insist on "Helping" these people who will eventually become permanent, fulltime, nonproductive members of our society. Again, the question is asked, "Why?" Doesn't it seem strange that our government would continue to expand programs that are detrimental to its citizens and to society in general? What positive outcome has ever come from providing long-term

"Assistance" to any able-bodied American? How many third generation welfare recipients will ever run for president or start a successful business, or even simply become self-sufficient? How many success stories do you hear coming from the projects and communities of subsidized housing around the country? If necessity is the mother of invention, I'd like to offer that entitlement is the mother of complacency.

I digress. We were talking about free and reduced school meals. So, what happens when school is out and the little kiddies are still hungry because their parents don't know the difference in responsibility between school months and summer months? Have no fear… the government is here.

Summer lunch programs are even more absurd and unnecessary than are school lunches. Think about the absurdity of feeding kids at a skate park, a public pool or a park playground. If the kids are able to cover the entrance fee to a pool or skate park, how are they unable to obtain lunch? I know, I know. How can you ask a kid to choose between summer fun and a meal? I don't think the kid *should* have to choose. That should be the parent's job! If the parents are so destitute that they can't provide food for their children then how in the world can they shell out three or four bucks so the kids can swim or skate?

During the summer of 2004 there were three million children who received summer lunches at nearly 30,000 sites across America. Although the number of kids receiving summer lunches is currently just a fraction of those children receiving free meals during the school year, things are changing. The push to attract more children to the sites where summer lunches are distributed is under way. Kids are being recruited by the kind-hearted directors and organizers of the summer lunch programs in hopes that the service numbers will soar and more funding can then be made available for these needy children.

I didn't know it, but last summer I found out that my own son was a "Needy" child. That's right. Although my wife and I are both professionals, my son was fed a federally reimbursed summer lunch at the community pool. This is what happened. My son (15 at the time) and two of his friends went to the community pool one day in July to enjoy a couple hours of swim time. A few hours later he and his friend came to the house to change and go play. My wife and I asked if they were hungry and if they'd like us to fix them some lunch. They all said, "No, we ate lunch at the pool." We'd given them money to swim but no extra for goodies at the snack bar. "How did you buy lunch at the pool," we asked. "We didn't buy it, there were these people down there giving out free bag lunches to all the kids at the pool. We had to eat them in the pool area and they just handed them out to everyone." My wife and I knew immediately that he was referring to the free lunches that were intended to be distributed to low-income kids who already received free or reduced school lunches. The summer lunch program staff at the pool also told the children receiving these lunches to, "Tell your friends to come down tomorrow for a free lunch." I asked what kind of questions they asked the kids before they received their lunch. I expected them to say that questions about free/reduced school lunches or food stamps had come up, but no questions were asked. No proof of being low-income was required. No verification of eligibility was requested.

These kind-hearted folks had just put my kid on the government dole. When I asked him, he said he didn't feel weird about taking a free lunch because the people giving them out, "Just invited everyone over to get one." Here we go again trying to make freebies acceptable and remove any stigma associated with receiving something for nothing. If we can normalize this behavior amongst the children in our society, what will we have to look forward to as this generation of new "Recipients" grows up? With no shame or dignity (or even a concept of them) we can expect their generation to take advantage of the government assistance programs at a much greater rate than folks do today. Mission accomplished, again!

Now I don't know how many of the kids at the pool that day were eligible for free summer lunches but I know for a fact that three of them weren't. I'd be willing to bet that no more than two, three or maybe four out of ten were. That is a huge abuse rate. It is unconscionable that those in charge of the distribution not only failed to be sure the kids qualified for the "Service," but they were actively recruiting kids by telling them to invite their friends to come for a free lunch.

How am I supposed to support a program that refuses to use any means testing? Why would I want to pay money to feed the children of doctors, lawyers and other professionals every day during the summer months? How can my tax dollars be squandered so blatantly and no action be taken to remedy the abuse? Why should my child, who has all the privileges that a responsible parent should provide their children, be allowed to eat food designated for a truly needy child? This is where your tax dollars go and this epitomizes the misuse of "Government dollars." This is one reason why we're required to pay more taxes every year.

It's been made to look like a complex, difficult problem that requires brilliant minds and countless government agencies to address. Hungry kids cost the country *billions* of dollars each year. The bureaucracy that both created the problem initially, and now claims to be solving it, is a monster business that employs hundreds of thousands of people. We've created Mount Everest out of an anthill and overlooked the most simple and basic solution to a problem that we've not only created, but also encouraged. Want to know how to feed hungry kids regardless of the time of year? Here's what we need to say! *Parents*...get your ass out of bed and cook breakfast for the children you brought into this world. When your done cooking breakfast for you kids, pack them a lunch to take to school or to the park. There it is. It costs no more than the food stamps they already receive and with this advise, followed to the letter, no child will ever be hungry! We must quit making excuses for these folks and start demanding personal responsibility.

## MORE FREE FOOD

Food banks in America are billed as the safety net for the safety net. They are able to supply additional food to those receiving food stamps. They can feed those who don't qualify for food stamps and they can distribute food to those who have fallen through the cracks or been bounced around by red tape.

Food bank programs across the country all differ in some minor ways but most run very similarly. In most cases, USDA commodities are often associated with food banks and some still refer to it as the "Government cheese program." Although the cheese supply has long been exhausted, the government supplies numerous other food items to non-profit agencies that distribute food to those in need. As subsidies to America's farmers continue and increase, food banks see a variety of quality food products being offered to them. Unfortunately the quality and quantity of these products are just too much for food banks to refuse and that has become the ultimate reason private food banks are now in danger of failing. I'll talk more about that in a minute. Coupled with the commodity food *supplied by the government* (Is this starting to sound like a story from the Russian AP wire?) food banks rely heavily on food retailers, wholesalers, manufactures and distributors to collect food products for distribution.

These are often products that may have been slightly damaged during shipping, that may be close to the "Pull-date," are recently expired, or have been deemed not up to snuff for retail sale due to packaging or some other minor defect. Funding to pay for hugely discounted food and for the cost of transporting the millions of tons of food each year, is largely raised in the private sector. Charitable foundations, service organizations and private citizens comprise the majority of funding for most non-profit food banks. A comparatively small staff and a large corps of volunteers allow food banks to distribute huge amounts of food while incurring minimal cost. These products are banked in different states and different regions and distributed to direct service agencies, the majority of which are church organizations. (Church organizations that take care of their families, friends and neighbors. Ring any bells?) This system of private citizens and organizations raising money to obtain food to be distributed to those in need by church organizations is a wonderful and cost-effective way to address hunger. But let's not forget that the government has thrown its two cents into the private assistance sector.

That's where things go awry. Any private assistance organization the government vows to "Assist," is destined to fail. Unfortunately, an otherwise efficient food bank system has been no exception. Once a food bank decides to accept USDA commodities, their ability to run a food pantry with common sense and efficiency is taken away. The ability to prioritize need among those seeking assistance is removed. Also lacking is the pantry's ability to address and fix any abuse of services, as long as they receive commodity food.

Once commodities are accepted, Civil Rights training is required of all staff and volunteers, who have been distributing food (in some cases for years or decades) with no previous training or problems. Nobody can require a food recipient to show proof that they meet the USDA-determined income guidelines. Nobody who self-declares that they meet the guidelines can be refused food. In other words, once the government starts "Helping" the private sector, food banks become a politically correct, and eventually, defunct business.

Lets look at what this means. As a result of political correctness, those receiving help are now referred to as "Clients." To refer to them as "Recipients" or "Needy" or "Hungry folks" is taboo. The last time I checked, a client was defined as a customer or patron. To receive a free service makes you neither. But to abide by our ultra-ridiculously over-sensitive way of treating anybody who asks for assistance, we now call them "Clients."

Also, as a stipulation of receiving USDA food, staff and volunteers can no longer use common sense to prioritize need among those receiving assistance. This means that all "Clients" that walk into a food bank must be treated equally. No more and no less assistance can be given due to age, employment status, disabilities, willingness to help ones self, or any other reason. Therefore, a twenty-five year old single man who chooses not to work is guaranteed to receive the same amount of food in a food box as an eighty-five year old widow living on a $400 a month fixed income. Civil Rights and an enforced avoidance of common sense has insured that the "Government way" is now reflected in private sector assistance programs. Likewise, a family with two parents that don't work, and a couple of kids no longer in school but still living at home, who have been receiving food assistance each month for three years, is assured ongoing assistance, even if that assistance reduces the amount of help another individual or family may need. This policy of blind equality has reduced the quantity and quality of assistance one gets upon receiving a food box. Eventually the system will be so watered down that any assistance will be next to meaningless.

Where once recipients were simply humble and thankful for assistance, many food banks have instituted a "Client's Rights Policy." This allows any disgruntled "Client" to file a discrimination complaint with the United States Department of Agriculture any time he or she feels their food box is too small or doesn't contain the items they demand. The "Clients" have more say in what goes into their food box now than do the volunteers and employees putting them together. How's that for "Client's rights?"

Talk about taking a perfectly functioning food assistance system, mixing in a dash of government "Support," and coming out with a completely dysfunctional system that helps too few while being governed by too many. The private sector had it figured out and the government figured out how to unravel it. I love it when the government gets involved to make things "Better."

# CHAPTER 6
# SCHOOLS, KIDS AND ENTITLEMENT

---

As a parent of three boys who were "Educated" in America's public school system, I have a very strong opinion of today's educators and the system they work for. Groups like The National Education Association (NEA) and American Federation of Teachers have worked so diligently for teacher's rights that now teachers have more rights than the parents and students who are at the mercy of the system. Public opinion of these once respected teachers has been tarnished as a result. In fact, teachers have found themselves the new butt of jokes and the target of criticism from dissatisfied parents of kids in the public school system. They are more distained and less respected than ever before. And why shouldn't they be?

As little as thirty years ago schoolteachers acted like responsible, respectable, honorable, caring, moral, concerned educators to millions of school students in America. In my experience, teachers were pillars of our communities and were respected by everyone. Their goal back then was to teach children the basic educational foundation they'd need to be successful. They took pride in the outcomes of their students and were genuinely concerned about their progress and achievements. Teachers used to be proud of their profession and felt honored to be in charge of providing an education to their students. Money was secondary to outcome. Salary disputes were secondary to teaching. Benefits were secondary to a smart, well-behaved class and negotiations over summer vacation "Time off" were secondary to test scores.

There was a time when teachers showed up to school early to make themselves available to students who needed a little extra help or who had questions about their previous night's homework. They also stayed after class to assist students having trouble with a given concept or problem. Teachers worked on their grade books in class when their students were studying or took them home after work to figure grades. Teachers took control of their classrooms and seldom tolerated ill-behaved students. Classrooms were of a manageable size with a student to teacher ratio that was conducive to learning. Standards were high and goals were met, even exceeded, instead of continually lowered. Tests were considered a good way to gauge a student's comprehension of a given subject. Physical education was seen as a good way for kids to burn off some energy and stay physically fit. There was always one Principal and usually one Vice-Principal at each school be it an elementary school, a middle school, or a high school. Front office staff usually consisted of a school secretary, a school nurse, an attendance office attendant, a janitor or two and three or four people in the school cafeteria.

School hours used to be consistent and substantial. Topics of study were uniform and addressed the major subjects needed by children to build a good educational foundation. The primary focus of a school was to educate rather than employ. A few determined and caring teachers were worth ten times the administrative bureaucrats who are now in charge of "Educating" our children.

Adults who were fortunate enough to have started their education thirty or more years ago can all tell you who a favorite teacher was and why they were a favorite. Memories of school were memories of pencils, paper, classrooms, chalkboards, lunchrooms and schoolbooks as opposed to today's students that remember only fashions, the name brands of popular clothes or shoes and which students had the most expensive car. Memories of favorite teachers are now replaced with memories of favorite school party places. More focus is now put on who has the baggiest pants and coolest Discman than on who has the best class grade. Respect is given to the smart-ass punks who disrupt class instead of to the teachers in front of the class. The class delinquent, (who is as likely to carry a weapon to school as he is a notebook) has replaced the class clown. School sports are on the chopping block as funding is sought for on-campus student daycare centers and campus police officers. Music programs are nearly extinct, as classes dealing with homosexuality and tolerance have emerged. School dress codes are reminiscent of a Hollywood "Gangsta" rap video instead of a clean-cut businesslike attire that would be preferred in a learning atmosphere. Our upstanding young men are wearing ripped jeans sagging halfway down their butts with boxer shorts hanging out and t-shirts with offensive phrases or images on them. Our young ladies are in torn short skirts and shamefully skimpy tops and look more like truck stop prostitutes than students on junior high and high school campuses. And imagine all of this happening at a time in our country's history when a teenage girl can't legally be given an aspirin in school for a headache, but can be given an abortion (without parental notification) for a pregnancy.

Of course jocks are still jocks and nerds are still nerds. But the days of a jock simply giving the nerds a "wedgie" has been replaced by violent acts of sodomy being perpetrated on unsuspecting fellow students with broomsticks and baseball bats. The cheerleaders are now being drugged and raped at parties by the quarterback who used to ask them to the prom. Loners who once stayed to themselves now dress in all black and terrorize campuses with plots of school shootings and mass murder. Teachers are afraid to take control of their classrooms and have been taught to ignore or tolerate students who act disruptively in class. Bullies who used to steal a fellow student's lunch money are now threatening to kill teachers who discipline them. Apparently flipping off the American flag is more popular than saying the Pledge of Allegiance in many of today's classrooms. Classroom discussions of abortion, gay sex and social tolerance have replaced discussions of history, science and mathematical theory. Campuses are more of a social gathering place than an educational institution and anyone determined to learn is ridiculed by fellow students and ignored by teachers and administrators.

Why have schools gone from centers of learning to cesspools of juvenal delinquent daycare? Because parents aren't parenting, teachers aren't teaching and administrators aren't administrating. It is a combination of these things that has left the last few generations of American children undereducated and utterly ill prepared to face life in the real world.

Parents are too wrapped up in their own lives, their own problems or their own careers to spend time raising children with the love and discipline they need. The children grow up being spoiled with money and material objects while their poor behavior and grades are overlooked. This is the "Favor" done for children as Mom and Dad try to assuage their guilt over being neglectful parents. Gifts and tolerance on the part of the guilt-ridden parent inevitably leads to children who are misbehaved spoiled brats who learn to expect, rather than to work for what they want. They demand, instead of apply themselves and that translates to a poor attitude for any student. The entitlement mentality is instilled in today's todlers and continues with them as they grow until they reach school. By this time kids are pretty much used to getting what they want without having to work to obtain it. In the classroom they have none of the skills that they need to apply in order to accomplish a task. The grades reflect their lack of effort and we have entire grade levels receiving failing or near failing grades. How do our teachers and administrators deal with this problem? The easiest way they can. They lower standards and expect less from students. Where as a 50% score used to indicate a failing grade, it now indicated that a student has a "Fair" comprehension of a topic. I guess these administrators are taking an optimists stance on education. Where fifty percent used to indicate a student got half of the answers wrong, it now happily implies that the student actually got half of the answers correct. There is now a reward for getting half the answers correct. It breaks down something like this. Where as 100% used to equal an "A" and 50% translated to an "F", with seventy-five percent being the middle and equaling a "C", today's standards indicate 100% an "A", 0% an "F" with fifty percent being the middle and equaling a "C".

This situation has been perpetuated by the cause and effect cycle that inevitably follows the lowering of standards. Teachers have lost their teaching skills as a result of kids not being required to learn. It's gone on long enough now that neither the teachers nor the students walk into the classroom with an expectation that education will actually occur there. I know for a fact that any teacher that expects much of anything from his/her students is labeled a hard-ass and usually ends up in multiple parent-teacher meetings to explain why little Johnny is failing his class. After time, either the administration tells the teacher to ease the curriculum or the teacher tires of being scrutinized by angry parents who just *know* Johnny is smarter than the teacher is giving him credit for. Either way, after time, standards are lowered and the dumbing-down of our bright little minds occurs at all grade levels.

Kids are hard to teach because parents don't prepare them for school, or life in general. It's entirely the fault of the parent for the child being ill prepared. That being said, let's look at today's teachers, administrators, and unions and the problems they cause in our public education system.

The National Education Association (Americas biggest teacher's union) and the American Federation of Teachers, have been instrumental in shaping the new education system. The shape that it's taking is not only dangerous to the future of our children, but to the future of our country. The NEA is nothing more than a left wing lobbying group that has gained in power and in numbers, supporting ideas that push the Liberal agenda to the edge. For some time now the NEA has supported numerous liberal ideas such as "Gay and Lesbian Studies" and…surprise, surprise… they support radical feminism. They oppose school prayer and fight against any mention of religion in the classroom. They're supportive of reparations for slavery and promote multiculturalism in a time of terror.

These are the folks pushing the Liberal agenda that is being forced down the throats of our public school students. It starts when they are young and influential and continues as they grow into malleable teens. As only a small percentage of these students have parents who are socialist radicals, it's amazing how much power the NEA must have to continue to promote these leftist ideas. They make the educational process itself a social experiment that instills sensitivity and tolerance instead of grammar and science. They use the time we're forced to send our children away to their schools to indoctrinate them into Liberalism. It's no wonder the NEA viciously opposes the idea of school vouchers where morality, prayer and education would be promoted. This would really jeopardize their perfect assembly line-like brainwashing operation. They've simply worked too hard getting a socialist agenda into the schools to be undermined by a program where the goal is to educate American kids. Smart kids after all, grow to be responsible, self-supportive, productive, achieving, successful members of society. This is a society Liberals have been striving to bring down for decades and represents all that the NEA despises. It's time we tell the NEA to back off! Our children's futures, as well as the future of our country, hang in the balance.

We now know the agenda behind the teachers union. Now let's take a look at the teachers themselves. No longer is teaching a passion. The desire to instill knowledge in young minds and then watch it blossom throughout a school year (or years) used to be the primary reason for a teacher to enter the profession. Over time, changes have taken place in the public school system and teachers no longer care about their students as much as they care about their salaries and benefits. Teaching has gone from a self-fulfilling career to a moneymaking profession. With a national average salary of $46,600.00 in the 2003-2004 school year (according to the AFT), it would seem teachers have little to complain about. As the rest of us work 52 weeks a year to earn our living of a little more or a little less than a teacher's salary, educators put in an average of thirty-five weeks a year for their pay. This reflects the average 12-week summer break, 2-week Christmas (Oops, Winter Holiday) break, 1-week Thanksgiving break, and 1-week Easter (Oops, Spring) break.

This doesn't include the countless days that teachers don't teach due to grade preparation days off, teacher's in-service days, late school starts, early release days and countless other days given off for one reason or another. As an example, my sixteen-year-old son, who is a sophomore at a south central Oregon high school, has a schedule so ridiculous it almost seems to be a joke. School hours are listed in the school handbook as beginning at 7:55 am and dismissing at 3:05 pm. E*xcept*…..every Wednesday school starts at 9:35am to allow for some sort of teacher meetings. Wednesday also has a dismissal time of 2:30 for allowing teachers more time to do whatever they do at the expense of my son's education. Thursday also finds teachers letting the kids out at 2:30 instead of the regular time of 3:05. This is my son's weekly schedule. He only actually attends 3 full days of school per week and is short changed nearly 3 hours of classroom time weekly to accommodate teacher's meeting time. This doesn't include the full Friday that his teachers get off following each 6-week grading period, supposedly to assign grades to the students. These are certainly not three-day weekends used by our responsible educators for golf in the spring and fall or for skiing in the winter. No, no, no, these are days when the teacher sits down at home in the peace and quiet of their living room and evaluates each student.

Even when teachers *are* in class they do little to really educate our kids. My wife and I have held numerous meetings with teachers, principals and vice-principals over the course of our children's educational years. Reasons varied, but a few of the highlights are as follows.

    1)    Several years ago our oldest son came home from his freshman English class proud

of a "B+" paper he'd completed that week. Upon looking at the two-page paper, we noticed more than a dozen spelling errors and numerous punctuation errors. We wondered how a student could get such a high grade in English for a paper that showed he didn't really comprehend the use of the language. We contacted his English teacher and he informed us that he simply didn't have time to go through 105 papers and correct each spelling and grammar error. He informed us that he graded purely on content and to do otherwise might stifle the "Writers" imagination. After my wife and I wiped the dumbfounded looks off our faces, I asked him if he was indeed the "English" teacher, and if he was, he certainly wasn't helping my son learn English by ignoring punctuation and spelling errors. He continued on with some other unintelligible gibberish, but by that time I was done listening. I wanted to talk to the Principal. After a more official runaround with him we were told that it's up to the individual teacher on how to approach the curriculum and subject matter of a course. We didn't take the next step of going to the school board on this particular issue, but we did start correcting all of our son's papers at home. Why in the hell send a kid to English class if learning English is not in the curriculum? Isn't that like sending a student to math class but not pointing out addition errors?

2)      Our youngest boy was a freshman in high school when he was warned by one of his teachers not to wear a particular shirt to school again. My son asked why he couldn't wear the shirt and the teacher gave him no answer. My wife and I looked at the shirt and saw nothing offensive about it. We sent him back to school later that week in the same shirt and told him to find out why that teacher wouldn't allow it. The shirt in question had a cartoon picture of a monkey eating a banana and holding a beverage, which the teacher interpreted to be an alcoholic beverage. After informing him of his interpretation of the cartoon the teacher sent him home for wearing it again. My wife and I both agreed that representation of booze on a shirt worn to school was unacceptable. We simply didn't interpret the beverage as an alcoholic drink but told our boy to get rid of the shirt all the same. The problem here is that the very same teacher who sent my son home for wearing a shirt of a carton monkey, allowed other horrendous attire and foul behavior in his class. My son informed us (and we confirmed with a visit to his class) that several students dressed in "Necklaces" made of thick tow chains

secured to their necks by a pad lock. These kids also looked like pin cushions and displayed piercings in every imaginable area of their faces. Trench coats that were against the school dress code (for safety reasons related to concealing weapons) were displayed in the teacher's classroom. Pants were literally falling off of two male students and females showing more skin than a Saturday night HBO movie, were more common than not. One girl dressed in all black with black lipstick and eyeliner refused to stand during the weekly Pledge of Allegiance and flipped off the American flag while other students recited the words. But by God, my boy was wearing a shirt with a cartoon monkey that *might* have had an alcoholic beverage in has hand. There seemed to be no rhyme or reason to the teachers actions so we requested a meeting with the principal.

Before the meeting we referred to the student handbook and found that the representation of drugs, alcohol and tobacco on student clothing was a no-no. Good. We also noted in the handbook that the dress code did not allow baggy clothing, skimpy dress that revealed bra straps or midriffs, trench coats, or "Distractive" jewelry. When confronted with the fact that all of these violations were noted during a 10 minute visit to our son's classroom, the Vice-Principal told us his main concern was for student safety and that dress code rule were somewhat flexible. Basically he told us as long as kids were safe they could wear clothes that "expressed" their individuality. Great! Then what's wrong with a cartoon monkey? And why are kids getting away with wearing chains with padlocks that can be used as weapons? More common sense at work in our nation's schools. If these administrators can't apply common sense to an issue as simple as this, how can we possibly trust them with the education of our children?

3) Shortly before writing this chapter, my wife got a call from our sophomore's school counselor. He informed us that after looking at his records, he realized that our son was taking a math class he'd already had his freshman year. The name of the class had been changed but the content was basically the same. Also, a math credit couldn't be issued for repeating the class. Therefore, our boy (an honor roll student since 7th gradc) would be a year behind in meeting his college prerequisite in math. Before my wife had a chance to digest this information or pass the facts on to me, the counselor told my wife that there were two options to get him

caught up. He could either take two advanced math classes his senior year (very difficult) or we could pay to send him to a junior college summer school class to make up for the lost year of study. My wife was a bit confused with the whole situation and told the counselor that she'd talk to me and I'd get back to him. Well, once I heard about all of this I came unglued! I got back to him the next morning at 7:30am. He was a bit shocked to see me waiting for him at his office door and I might add, I was more than a little upset. Claiming not to have time to talk to me, he turned me over to one of the Assistant Principals. He briefly filled the A.P. in on the counseling error that cost my son a year of math requirements. I then told him that the two options given to us to get my son caught up were simply unacceptable. I demanded that the problem be fixed immediately at whatever means necessary and if it wasn't, feathers were going to fly. The tape recorder I held insured that no more excuses would be used to cover for their incompetence and my firm, slightly aggressive demeanor insured my point would be heard. The A.P. obviously told the Principal of his rather unpleasant meeting with a disgruntled father and we were contacted a half an hour after I left the school offices. The Principal offered tutoring classes to get my boy caught up on the necessary math skills and guaranteed his immediate placement in the correct math class. He also apologized for me having to come in to resolve yet another problem in the short time (2 years) that my youngest boy had attended his school. My point here is that a well paid high school counselor neglected to put my son in the correct math class his freshman year, and then placed him in the exact same class the following year. My son's college future depends on his performance in high school. He's met every goal and has attained excellent grades but his educational future has been put in jeopardy by a careless buffoon claiming to be a student "Counselor." To top it off the idiot told us that *we'd* have to pay to get him caught up. Like this was somehow our fault? Just another example of why it's so important to keep a close eye on those in charge of your kids' education. Hold them accountable and demand that they do their job right.

Once a teacher becomes a teacher, the union insures that short of rape or murder, he or she is just about immune to being fired or even severely reprimanded for what is sometimes appalling behavior. Teachers in our public schools get away with sexual harassment, belittling students, imposing their political beliefs on students and neglecting their duties as teachers, among other things. As they feel increasingly untouchable by anybody demanding responsibility and accountability, their teaching practices become lax. Their attitude towards the students and the parents becomes nonchalant. They've grow accustom to the short hours, long vacations and relaxed classroom atmosphere that the NEA has worked so hard to give them over the years.

They have not, though, grown accustomed to their "Low wages." Therefore, as Americans we are constantly bombarded with media interviews of teachers whining about low salaries, of school administrators complaining of small annual raises and of school board members bitching about funding issues. The NEA is forever in the spotlight preaching to us what a shame it is that we don't treat our teachers better. They continually lobby for pay increases. These folks fail to acknowledge that private schools in America provide a far better education to our children while spending up to fifty percent less per student than public schools.

In my son's school district a total of ten thousand dollars per student is allocated to his school each year. Local private schools spend about five thousand. Could it be that my son's school, with its huge administrative payroll, might be too top heavy? Does a school of fewer than a thousand students require more than one Principal and two Vice-Principals? Couldn't the duties of all of these administrators be consolidated and delegated to one or two head honchos? How much money would be saved if we cut the supporting positions of three Vice-Principals? The assistant Vice-Principal could go, as could the assistant *to* the Vice-Principal *and* the Vice-Principals assistant's assistant. Then there are the secretaries to the Principals and Vice-Principals and the secretaries to assistants to both the Principal and Vice-Principal's assistants. Confused yet? The NEA hopes so. The more positions they can fill at your public school, the more money they can demand for "Education." Never mind that virtually none of those additional funds will trickle down to the classrooms in order to provide new desks, art or shop supplies, to fund music or sports programs, or upgrade dilapidated school buildings. No, no, no, these funds are divvied up first among the school administrators and then what's left is doled out to teachers in the form of raises. Could it be that by private schools having only the *necessary* administrators to efficiently run a school, money can actually be used to educate students? Perhaps this is a concept the teachers unions should be made aware of. Maybe they're already aware and maybe it's the reason they so vehemently oppose the idea and implementation of the school voucher system. What do you think?

As we've seen, students feel entitled to be educated without having to apply themselves, as if knowledge is owed to them and can be instilled in them by simply sitting in a classroom for five or six hours a day. Teachers are entitled to long vacations, while lowering student standards and neglecting their duties as educators. They also feel entitled to a lot more than the paltry $46,600 dollars they make on average for working less than eight months per year. Administrators feel entitled to make more than double what a teacher "Earns," while having at their disposal plenty of support staff to assist in their job of overseeing the defunct school system they are in charge of.

Nobody is willing to work. At least not willing to work hard to become educated. Not willing to work hard to educate, and not willing to work hard to efficiently run a school system that has become utterly ineffective and wasteful. Entitlement, as related to education, has ensured a place for American students nearly equivalent to those being educated in third world countries. Our graduates are functionally illiterate, ill prepared to fill out a job application and even less prepared to perform basic job skills. "Graduates" are unable to solve problems that require anything but basic math and reasoning skills and they're unintelligent enough to think that because they received a diploma, they actually earned it.

# CHAPTER 7
# PARENTS ARE A PROBLEM

Mom. The kind, caring, nurturing, soft spoken woman who was always there to help you along and patch up your scrapes when you fell.

Dad. The supportive, encouraging, mentoring disciplinarian who pushed us to be better and helped us achieve that goal.

Ozzie and Harriet and Leave it to Beaver might have been a bit simplistic during their time and are surely even more so today, but the families portrayed in those shows reflected the typical American family in days gone by. The basic family unit was intact and parents were a part of their kid's lives. Being a parent didn't stop at giving birth. The responsibilities associated with raising children were well known and taken seriously. Parents took pride in raising a child who grew to be a good student, respectable member of the community and later, a successful adult. This was the rule and not the exception.

Then came the 1960's and we can watch the family unit deteriorate from there. We can find many reasons for the slow but steady demise of family structures and values. We can look at some of the negative effects that civil rights had on African American families as time progressed. We can see the result feminism had on American families, as women increasingly took jobs outside the home. We can see how moral decay has led to generations of misbehaved and increasingly violent young people. And we can see the effects entitlement programs have had on families that used to be independent and proud.

Most importantly, we can see the affects of parents shunning their parental responsibilities and becoming increasingly detached from the lives of their children.

Too many American parents are ill prepared to take on the role of Mom or Dad when they start a family. No longer do responsible married couples work hard to save and prepare for a family. No savings, no supplies, no room in the house, no funds set aside for the child's future. No idea of what it takes to raise a child emotionally, physically, or financially. In today's world a family is usually started when a wife (or girlfriend, or a female acquaintance) becomes pregnant. It is seldom planned and rarely expected. If the parents are lucky enough to be married and are somewhat financially stable, then some hope remains for the child. If not, few kids are able to overcome the odds of being brought into a world by parents who didn't even intend to create a child in the first place. Figure on top of that the ages at which parents are having children and we can see that in essence, our youth are having babies. Full student daycare centers on America's high school campuses attest to the effectiveness of today's sexually tolerant teachings. Obviously pushing rubbers and birth control on our teens has worked to great success.

Anyone can "Make a mistake," but the rate at which these mistakes are being made is alarming to say the least. Kids simply aren't taught about responsibility and about the consequences of their actions at an early age. And why would they be taught? After two or three generations of poor parenting being passed on from generation to generation, Mom and Dad simply don't know how to be parents anymore. This leads us to the current generation's unofficial motto of "Do it if it feels good." It doesn't matter if it's stealing, doing drugs, picking on others, having sex, or dropping out of school. If it feels right, then it must be okay. We're reaping the behavior of kids who didn't have involved parents.

Parents today are too busy with their own lives to be involved in the lives of their kids. Two parent families, in which both parents work full time, are often as dysfunctional as single parent families. In today's world, a person's identity is based on what that person does for a living. Those who are titled Doctor, Lawyer, Executive or Professor earn prestige. This is pure selfishness on the part of the parent. Pride and prestige should be judged not in how much money you earn each year, but how your family learns, grows, and functions each day. Parents who work eight hours a day usually have time to spend with their children, if they choose to. Many choose not to and use excuses like, "Work wiped me out, I need my rest," or "Feed yourself tonight, I'm beat." We all have bad days, but when we use these excuses every day, our children are neglected and our families drift apart. When parents show no interest in their children, kids look for attention elsewhere and it often comes from activities or people that don't have the child's best interests in mind.

It's to the point now that many young parents have absolutely no idea what being a parent means. The whole concept of what a parent is and does has been so watered down that the duties of a parent have to be explained to young mothers or couples in "Parenting" classes. When children have to face such disadvantages at such an early age, they simply have no hope of being raised the way a child deserves to be raised. As a result, we have an aging group of kids who generally take no responsibility for their actions because they've never been taught that actions have consequences. They have no drive to be successful because they were never taught to set goals or how to achieve them. They don't know how to support themselves because they've always relied on others to support them. These kids can't do well in school because their parents never helped them learn how to study. As they grow up, they can't hold jobs because they never learned to be reliable, responsible or dependable. And they turn out to be lousy parents because they never had an example to learn from when they were growing up! Therefore, when they have kids, the cycle perpetuates itself, but seems to get exponentially worse.

One way that neglectful parents "Make up" for not spending time with their kids is to spoil them rotten with money and material items. From ice cream and candy bars to outrageous allowances and cars, parents often make the mistake of giving, while requiring nothing of the children in return. We can all look around and see a misbehaved little fat kid sucking on a lollipop while mom pays him no mind because she's busy with her own thing. We can see a teenager who can't pass basic math and English classes, but drives a new car that daddy bought him. There is no sense of ownership for these kids when their parents just keep giving them what they want in an effort to ease their own guilt over poor parenting. Excuses like, "I can't go to Junior's baseball game again this weekend because I'm working overtime," or "I promise that I'll make it to your next dance recital," are all too often atoned for with a nice gift being bought for the child. Parents neglect to realize that no amount of money or gifts will make up for broken promises and time lost together. Some otherwise seemingly intelligent people I know fail to see that they're doing their kids no favors by supplementing gifts for their attention.

These kids learn early how to manipulate their folks to get more gifts and material items. Soon, Mom and Dad have bought the kid everything he wants and can't understand why he's still not happy. In rebellion or as a way to get the parent's attention, kids act up or get into trouble at school. Their behavior worsens until the parents *have* to take notice of the child and then try to find an easy fix for their kid's behavior. It might be putting the kid on Ritalin or sending him to a shrink. This just confuses the child and makes him second-guess his own self-worth and sanity. Way to go, folks!

These kids turn out to be the stereotypical "Spoiled brat," who grow up with all the perceived advantages, but are constantly in trouble with the law or becomes a lazy, unproductive individual. Either way, the parents are to blame for the child's outcome. Showering a kid who needs love, guidance and discipline with gifts, tolerance and freedom is simply asking for your kid to be screwed up. When will parents begin to understand that being a parent means they *must* take on the responsibility of parenting! Until they do, our society will continue to reflect the troubles that occur in far too many households every day.

Another fairly recent development we see in parents is the denial of their child's guilt regarding just about everything. Thirty years ago when a neighbor would tell your folks that you'd thrown a ball into his yard and broke a window, you'd be guilty before proven innocent. A parent would take responsibility for their kid's action and pay to replace the window and make the child apologize. More often than not, the kid would be an indentured servant to Dad until he'd mowed enough lawns or washed enough cars to cover the cost of the window. I remember these days and grew up with a respect for other peoples' property as well as being more aware of my surroundings, learning how to plan better and taking responsibility for my actions. Plus, I was a hell of a lawn mover and could wash a car in record time.

Unfortunately, parents today tend not to believe that the neighbor, who saw little Jimmy throw the ball through his window, is telling the truth. They claim the neighbor, "Must be mistaken," or even cover for the kid by lying. Occasionally, parents are so offended at someone accusing their perfect child of doing something wrong that they become agitated and aggressive towards the accuser. Standing up for a child by not acknowledging that he's done something wrong, is another way parents are encouraging their kids to misbehave and disrespect others. After all, if no consequences follow misbehavior the child must infer that the behavior wasn't bad. If it were bad he would be punished, right? Modern parents further confuse kids by showing their offense at the accuser for pointing the finger at their child. This tells the kids that by acting offended or getting angry they can divert the real issue by masking it with additional poor behavior until the original issue is dropped.

How does denying, or covering for their poor behavior, possibly teach our kids the respect and responsibility they need to be part of a civil and generally amiable society? Is it any wonder each generation takes less personal responsibility than the one before it? Might this explain why today's kids have little or no respect for others property and belongings? Would it be a stretch to conclude that today kids and young adults curse and fight and steal and fail more than any generation in our recent history?

What else do our lazy, uneducated, neglectful, or otherwise under-qualified parents do to put their kids at further disadvantage of being happy, healthy and successful? In their busy or self-absorbed lives, today Moms and Dads find another easy way out. This time it comes at the expense of the child's physical health. It's diet, or lack there of. The dining room table was once a place for family to eat, talk and bond. It's where we learned about what was going on in our family's lives. Dinner was usually at a set time. Cooking was done in the kitchen and family members helped Mom prepare the food and set table. Dinner almost always consisted of a meat dish or a casserole, vegetables, bread or pasta dish and maybe a salad. A slice of cake or pie was a nice treat a couple of times a week following the evening meal. Well-rounded meals provided the nutrition needed by growing kids and sustained them without overindulging them.

Things have changed so much in this department that a family meal for many families comes twice a year, at Thanksgiving and Christmas. The other 363 days a year children are fed at all hours of the day. They eat whatever is on hand and easy to stick in the microwave or boil in a pot. More often than not the kids prepare it themselves because their parents are absent or, "Too tied up at the moment" to be bothered with cooking chores. Since kids *do* tend to feed themselves these days, considerate parents stock up on easy to prepare, microwaveable, foods that are usually full of fat, low in nutrition and are full of empty calories. These are considered the responsible parents.

The ones who "Spoil" their kids pass them a ten-dollar bill and send them out to gorge on Big Mac's, Whoppers, Buckets of Chicken and Value Meals. Kids today are so grossly overweight that childhood diabetes and heart problems amongst our nation's youth are becoming an epidemic. Cholesterol and blood pressure are dangerously high among even grade school children.

I'm no nutrition expert, but any idiot with a pinch of common sense can look at the nutritional information at your favorite fast food joint and know that this food isn't good for you. The following information was taken from the official web sites of each respective restaurant. At McDonalds's a "Double Quarter Pounder w/Cheese" will cost you 730 calories and 40 grams of fat, add a large fry and pack away another 520 calories and 25 grams of fat. That's more than half of the recommended daily allowance (RDA) of both calories and fat.....If you only eat one burger and one large French fry. The same goes for Burger King where a "Triple Whopper" runs 1,230 calories and packs 82 grams of fat. Their "King-Size fries" will cost you an additional 600 calories and 33 grams of fat. How about a trip To Jack In The Box where you can have a "Bacon Ultimate Cheeseburger" for 1,090 calories and 77 grams of fat and enjoy an "Oreo Cookie Shake" for a whopping 1,350 calories and 66 grams of fat.

The calories and fat in fast food are not the only thing today's Kids are contending with. The sodium content also meets or exceeds the RDA suggested serving portions if only one of these burgers and a side of french fries are consumed. Unfortunately, our society has gluttonized its citizens over the years and has now convinced us if one is good and two is better, then three or four or five is perfectly acceptable. As a very active and athletic high school student I could eat ten Big Mac's (much to the disbelief of my best friend). I only did it a couple of times and McDonald's remained a treat and not a regular eatery. Thankfully age and common sense have deterred me from doing this anymore but today's kids are different. Kids eat at fast food places on an alarmingly regular basis. They also consume several "Dollar Menu" items or hugely oversized "Value Meals." This has led to overweight, lethargic kids who are more interested in their next meal than the activities that should be taking place between meals. How motivated would you be to go out and do something even remotely energetic if you'd just consumed three Whoppers with cheese, a large fry, a chocolate milk shake and a super-sized Coke... to the tune of about 4,000 calories and more than 250 grams of fat? That's why they plop down in front of video games or television instead of playing basketball at the local park or riding their bikes to the local pool or swimming hole.

I took an unscientific survey of twenty of my sixteen-year-old son's friends. They had different family backgrounds, athletic abilities and body types. I found that 15 out of the twenty I asked, eat at a fast food restaurant at least four days per week. Nine of those eat fast food daily and four eat fast food multiple times daily on a regular basis. This may be a small cross section of teenagers from a small town, but it certainly opened my eyes to the frequency young people eat at fast food establishments. There are serious dangers associated with this type of gluttony.

We're raising unmotivated, over fat, lazy, future Medicare dependents, and we're paying good money to the Fast Food industry to do it. Now I'm not saying it's McDonald's or Wendy's fault *at all*. They simply provide a service that modern day Americans can't resist. Everything in moderation, right? It may be laziness, a busy schedule, or a dozen other things, but regardless of the excuse, it's endangering the health of our kids and insuring their place in an early grave. In the past, generations of children learned cooking and nutrition skills from their parents. Kids still learn from their parents today, but unfortunately parents are teaching them about drive-thru's and value meals instead of grilling and steaming. As time progresses I'm afraid all the tradition of family meals and knowledge of cooking skills will be lost to fast food, as an even fatter and more lazy society emerges.

Parenting and the teaching of personal responsibility should go hand-in-hand. It's too bad that the concept has been so dulled and is now on the verge of being lost. It's a problem that is difficult to reverse and will be even harder to instill in parents-to-be, who simply never learned the concept from their own parents. How do geese learn the flyways (used to migrate south in the winter) if they don't learn it from their parents as young goslings? Without teaching our young, how can we expect them to survive and thrive?

It may be a Big Mac today, a poor report card tomorrow and a small crime next week. It doesn't look like much separately, but when we connect the dots we find a troubling scenario. The basic reason for a loose knit, dumbed-down society is a general lack of personal responsibility, both on the part of parents and children. As these kids grow, our political and societal leaders will lack personal responsibility just the same as our present (and future) professionals and laborers do. It's an epidemic and unchecked it will be the genesis to the downfall of our nation.

I guess it sounds cruel but it needs to be said; *Stupid people shouldn't breed!* If they'd just lay off all the frivolous procreation we *would* live in a world of higher standards, higher morals, integrity, self-sufficiency and strength. Unfortunately, minimal intelligence quotients and a basic understanding of the concept of common sense aren't prerequisites for parenting a child. Stupid people shouldn't breed…. Oh come on, I know you've thought it too.

# CHAPTER 8
# WE'RE NOT ALL THE SAME!

Contrary to what our liberal political leaders, school administrators, social service providers and legislative advocates would have you believe, we're not all the same. It seems that the new politically correct thing do is pretend that absolutely no differences exist between races, classes, intelligence, athleticism, determination, commitment, honesty, integrity, morality, or anything else that we all know separate one individual from another. Somehow being "The same" is being presented as the nice thing to do.

The idea of sameness is now being actively instituted. Our school system (as is usually the case) has proven to be the social testing grounds for this novel idea. One of the biggest examples that I can think of is the restructuring of the grading system to eliminate hurt feelings among students who receive a "Bad grade" due to poor performance. The intellectual asses who run and shape our public schools have been working diligently to change public perception of what letter grades actually represent. They've decided that rewarding good students with good grades and issuing low grades to poor students is cruel and intolerable. In some study in some back room of the education department of some liberal city like New York or San Francisco, researchers must have found that the only result of issuing poor students a low grade is irreversible psychological damage and ongoing low self-esteem issues. No longer does a "D" or an "F" on a report card say, "Hey kid, get on the ball and start applying yourself because you're doing poorly in this class." Too many excuses are made to save the feelings of children who simply don't apply themselves. As a result, they seldom live up to their true potential as students and later, as professionals or employees in our nation's work force.

What our intellectual counterparts describe as "Labeling," you and I call evaluating. That's what report cards do. They evaluate a student. A good grade indicates a student understands a given subject. A poor grade indicates that the student doesn't. It's that simple. Why quit giving bad grades to students who obviously don't understand the subject matter? Will changing an "F" to an "It's alright" or "Good try" on their report card change the fact that the student doesn't understand the subject matter? And why take away an "A" from a student who works hard to do well in the class? Does punishing the "A" student by not acknowledging his hard work help the "F" student they're coddling, feel better about himself? Why not just give all students the same grade, we'll say a "C" or a "You did pretty well" and lose the cruel and insensitive grading scale that rewards hard work and points out failure? Well, that's exactly what is being done in many schools around the country.

The grading system is one of the best examples demonstrating the movement to make all kids feel and act and be treated exactly as equals. It disallows any standouts, exceptional achievements, or efforts that go above and beyond to make a student stand apart from his or her peers. In fact extra effort is being discouraged because that student's achievement may make a less eager student feel inadequate. The administrator's opinion on this, "We won't have hurt feelings in any way shape or form in our schools!" It's to the point that any terminology or nomenclature that may possibly be inferred as the least bit derogatory or critical toward a poor student is being banned from our campuses.

To take it a step further, the use of red pens to point out errors on student's papers are being phased out and replaced by more subtle colors. Why? Because that bright red pen just screams, " MISTAKE!" Pardon me, but isn't that what teachers do? Point out mistakes so students can correct and learn from them? Why be subtle about letting a student know a word is misspelled or a math equation has been done incorrectly? Because a student with few or no red marks might be looked at as doing well, while a paper that looks like a murder scene may indicate that a student did poorly. We can't have a differentiation of students in schools. Again, it's not fair to the lesser students if their mistakes are pointed out, even if hard working students are denied acknowledgement for their achievements.

This idea of equality among all students is lowering the bar in our educational system. It works something like this. If seventy-five percent of the class understands the curriculum and twenty-five percent doesn't, then administrators will dumb-down the curriculum until the twenty five percent have at least a decent grasp on the subject. What does that do for the rest of the class? Allowing them to be complacent does nothing to expand either their understanding or knowledge. Hurting the top three quarters of the class to make the bottom quarter feel better about themselves is the new P.C. thing to do. Is it any wonder why American public school students are finding it hard to secure a good job after graduation? Is it any wonder the gap between the "Rich" and the "Poor" continues to widen? The intellectual pukes who encourage this system of educating our nation's youth are the same folks who whine about the rich getting richer and the poor getting poorer. These are the same folks who tell us to "Celebrate diversity" and then institute rules and regulations that smother individuality. Make any sense to you?

I suggest that a group of these ultra-intelligent poppas asses conduct a study on cause/effect or action/ reaction. Then, by seeing the actual study in front of them, they might understand how their brilliant educational ideas are causing our nation's youth to become less educated and therefore, less wealthy. What seems so simple to you and I has to be studied and analyzed by these self-proclaimed intelligent people. How sad that our society suffers as a result of their misguided social experiments!

How else have Liberals attempted to make us all the same? It just happens that this example *also* takes place in our nation's schools. It's not as widely spread as the grading issue yet, but given time, our thickheaded friends on the left will strive to institute this as well. What are they trying to alter? Sports.

Historically sports have been a part of public schools providing physical fitness, teaching teamwork and instilling a sense of pride and prestige to student bodies across the country. Bragging rights surrounding high school football, baseball, basketball, volleyball, soccer, wrestling and track teams are a part of any town's culture and are often a common thread and sense of pride for the entire community. How many small towns display signs saying, "Anytown, home of the state champion Tigers," or "Congratulations Anytown Warriors, district champs?"

Sports play an important role in the development of a well-rounded child. Sports teach kids how to work together to accomplish a goal. They promote physical fitness and teach kids the importance of health and exercise. Sports build self-confidence in kids and instill a sense of self-assurance. Sports teach kids to work hard to better themselves. Sports also teach humility and how to lose with grace. All of these are lessons kids learn and apply to situations they'll face later in life. Therefore, sports and team activities are in many ways as important as the reading, writing and 'rithmatic kids are supposed to be learning in our public schools.

In a veiled attempt to cut sports programs, with excuses of budget cuts and funding issues, our all-knowing bleeding heart Liberals are actively on the attack. Lately a few of these anti-sports yo-yo's have just come out and said what it is they're trying to do. They want to put an end to competitive sports and competitive events in our schools. To make all children equal, sports must be eliminated. With winners and losers in every competition and with such cruel institutions as All-Star teams and awards for standout players, equality simply can't be attained.

Liberals don't believe in labeling kids as "Winners" or "Losers" and certainly can't understand why scores must be kept and why competition must be competitive. Unlike life in the real world, Liberals are attempting to shelter our children from competition and rivalry, in essence, denying them the opportunity to learn the lessons they'll eventually need in life. They effectively discount the idea that the benefits sports instill, are more important than the emotional scars a child will be left with after losing a soccer or football game.

And *never* should there be acknowledgement for an exceptional athlete. A stand out athlete should not be recognized anymore than should a third string benchwarmer. Equality is more important than rewarding or even noticing the athlete who spends extra time in the gym or on the track to give himself the edge needed to be better than the competition. In fact, words like better and worse shouldn't even be used.

It sounds ridiculous because it is. The entire concept of denying our children the chance to compete in sports because they might feel bad if they lose is like denying food to a person because he might feel bad if he gains weight. Obviously the benefits of participating in sports and the benefits of eating far outweigh the "Risk" of having your feelings hurt as a result of the activity.

Maybe we should eliminate the eating of food on our school campuses. The argument could be that a skinny kid eating a Twinkie is cruel and insensitive to a student with a weight problem, not able to enjoy such treats. Those students who could afford a hot school lunch would offend the less fortunate students eating out of a brown paper sack. (Wait a minute; Liberals have already equalized that issue with the free and reduced lunch program.) Is it fair and equal that some kids eat pizza or fast food for lunch while others have cold sandwiches and crushed potato chips? I don't think so! Therefore, I suggest that food be removed from public schools and nobody be allowed to eat unless everybody eats the same type and the same amount of food each and every day. Never mind that studies show that kids who are fed have a higher learning curve and test scores. Don't let the fact that a lack of food results in a lack of concentration in the classroom. It's more important that kids don't feel offended or less fortunate than others at lunchtime.

Now that Liberals have snubbed the smart hard working students and the athletes who take pride in their sport, how else can they institute the "We're all the same" mentality on society? Well, they do it with social classes in America every day. They also try to make law-abiding citizens and criminals out to be just the same.

Let's first look at the "Have" and the "Have-not's" in society. First of all, with the way kids are brought up in our public school system, is it any wonder that our undereducated, functionally illiterate "Graduates" are under-performing and under-earning the rest of intelligent America? Class differentiation is a direct reflection of the education and determination of those who fit *into* a given class. Of course our Liberal yo-yo's feel labeling people by their class (low-income, middle class, rich, etc.) is highly offensive and altogether wrong. In fact, they don't believe that different classes should even exist. In their far out view of Utopia, Liberals believe all people should have exactly the same education, income, physical possessions and opportunities. They haven't yet realized that each individual is different (therefore the term individual.)

They neglect to acknowledge that not all of us are cut out to be a surgeon or a physicist. They deny that a surgeon or physicist should earn more money than a janitor or fast food employee. And most importantly, they are blind to the fact that opportunities are made and not just set in front of any and all individuals equally.

We know they choose to ignore these facts. Still, modern Liberals believe that a gap between those who are educated, determined, successful and wealthy, and those who are uneducated, unmotivated and therefore low-income, is designed by conservative politicians to keep the "Rich, rich and the poor, poor." It's not a conspiracy, and for anyone with common sense it's not hard to see why things are the way they are.

Regardless (or in spite of) the cause for the "Gap," the Left is working hard to close it. They're instituting policy that slowly but surely works to eliminate the ability for individuals to earn a lot of money. They overtax the wealthy in order to give tax refunds to the non-working. They continually advocate for the need to raise the minimum wage. They support living wage jobs regardless of what those jobs are.

Liberals want us all to be gainfully employed at medium paying jobs so everybody's paycheck is equal. This is not the American way of life. It goes against the idea that anyone can pull themselves up by the bootstraps and apply themselves to become successful and wealthy. Why work diligently to educate yourself, strive to be good at what you do, and take pride in your work if the guy next to you is making the same amount and is an uneducated slob who's happy with mediocre work and has no pride in his job?

There is an "Us and them" mentality in our society. It's real and it's to be expected. We're all humans and thus bipedal. After that, similarities between individuals start to become apparent. The closer we look, the more we see the differences of individuals in a country, a region, a city, a community, a neighborhood and even within a family. If family members with the same basic genetic makeup differ so vastly, how can liberals conceive that the citizens of a huge nation should think and act and behave and be treated as one? How rose colored are their glasses? Rosy enough to actually think this can be accomplished.

Our criminal justice system is another example of the Left working to make us all the same. We're told the same equality should be given to those who are law-abiding citizens and those who are convicted. As ridiculous and far out as this sounds, prisoner advocates, judges and even our nation's law makers are forcing an agenda to ensure certain rights to criminals. The same rights, in fact, afforded to honest lawful citizens of America. Murderers, child molesters, rapists, armed robbers and other highly dangerous social misfits are being insured the same rights as you and I, by groups like the ACLU.

In fact, it's funny how the rights of prisoners are actually more important than our rights when it comes a subject as basic as religion. We know the ACLU fights tooth and nail to remove Christ and Christianity from our society. Every December Christians are under attack from the ACLU for doing such dastardly things as saying "Merry Christmas," for displaying manger scenes in our parks and in our yards and by allowing our grade school kids to hold Christmas pageants. The same misguided group who believes Christianity has no place in American society changed it's tune when the religious rights of a Christian inmate in Rhode Island were recently violated. According to the ACLU's Prisoners' Rights web site, the ACLU of Rhode Island "Filed an appeal in federal court on behalf of a Christian prisoner who was barred from preaching during religious services at the state prison."

Why would an organization that despises Christianity defend the rights of a prisoner who wants to preach Christianity? Because the would-be preacher *is* a prisoner. You and I apparently have no right to openly express our Christian views, yet a convicted criminal who was denied his "Right" to preach in prison, has the very same organization who crushes our rights, support his. What a screwy bunch! In another case of "Lets treat criminals like everybody else," the ACLU fought to have the rights of a Jewish prisoner restored. The inmate's kosher diet was suspended as punishment after the inmate violated prison rules. An *inmate* who *violates* prison rules still gets to eat what he wants. I bet the inmate's victim is thrilled to know his/her attacker is eating well while being punished for his crime. What a relief to know that a prisoner's treatment is just as fair as the person who was violated.

Day to day life finds our violent offenders enjoying televisions in their cell, the use of weights and exercise equipment to keep them in top athletic shape, healthcare provided courtesy of our tax dollars and access to libraries and arts and crafts supplies. How nice. Let's not forget that the victims of these violent offenders have had their life taken or altered forever. *Their* rights sure weren't a consideration during the commission of the crime, yet we're expected to extend rights to felons who have taken the same rights from their victims. Common sense tells us that if you murder or rape or molest, that your constitutional rights should be forfeited. A big cost of freedom is personal responsibility. If you crave the former uphold the latter. If you don't, don't expect any extras, benefits, or condolences from the rest of us.

Why not give felons the right to vote. It is our right and a privilege to be able to take place in the political process that shapes our nation. A felon whose voting rights are revoked upon conviction, now have folks fighting for their rights to vote again. Florida has a 135-year-old law banning felons from voting. Due to the mention of "Racial discrimination," a Florida court is hearing a case on behalf of hundreds of thousands of felons who feel they should be allowed to vote. I sure hope that the group defending these felons doesn't suddenly adopt the idea that these folks should be allowed to carry guns again, too. Even our ex-president Hilary Clinton has stood up to support the voting rights of felons in New York. It's good to see that concern for violent criminals comes before the rights of the rest of Americans.

We see judges handing out ridiculously light sentences to criminals convicted of some pretty serious crimes, while at the same time a basic violation sometimes earn the guilty party a long stint in the county jail. We've all heard of child molesters who received a sixty-day sentence or a person convicted of murder receiving a fifteen-year sentence and getting out after eight years of "Good behavior." These folks are not the same as you and I. They have proven themselves to be capable of violent acts and have been convicted of perpetrating them on members of our society.

Why should they be treated with the same respect, dignity and granted the same rights (after committing an often violent crime) as the rest of us who may never have even a minor run-in with the law? Simply because it's the politically correct thing to do. I get mad when I hear folks say, "He's paid hid debt to society," or "He just made a mistake." I've never "Made a mistake" that's landed me in prison or cost another human being their life, yet I'm supposed to treat and be treated the same way as these criminals. That just doesn't set right with me! People should be looked at and judged according to their behavior and their treatment of others. If you've been rude and done harm to others, expect to be treated accordingly. If you've been law abiding and generally done the right thing throughout your life, then you should be treated accordingly. It's an easy concept to grasp for all but the wacko Left.

I'm just going to come out and say it. When it comes to skill level, intellectual capacity, morality, determination and ability, we're not the same! We never were and never will be! Some of us are better at what we do than others! Some people deserve to earn more money and some simply don't deserve the same pay as others! The ability to perform a job differs from person to person! Also, uneducated people will almost never go as far in life as educated individuals! There's a real and understandable reason for the gap between "Have and have-not's!" To try to make us all the same goes against the natural order of things. Just because a select few think it would be a nice concept and would make them feel all warm and fuzzy, doesn't mean it should, or even can be done.

# Chapter 9
# Our Kids Are Rude

Just look around a shopping mall on any given weekend and it's plain to see we're failing our children. Their behavior is rude, condescending, sarcastic, smart assed and more than all else...selfish.

It sounds clichéd, but the older I get the less I understand the behavior and attitude of our adolescents. I suppose it's nothing new for older Americans to be somewhat disappointed by the behavior of the younger generation. In fact, it's almost a tradition for parents to tell their kids how different things were when they were kids. Maybe I'm more critical than I should be, or maybe we haven't been nearly critical enough when it comes to the issue of our childrens behavior. I lean more towards the latter.

It's a fact that people interpret and judge you as a person based on the way you behave. Unfortunately, today's kids have such uniformly poor behavioral characteristics that it's hard for them to determine, even among themselves, who is acting poorly. It's becoming increasingly harder to differentiate between good kids and bad kids because their behavior varies to such a small degree.

As a society with a collective entitlement mentality, we've raised our kids to expect. Therefore, our kids are self-centered and truly believe the universe revolves around their wants, needs and problems. This is a dangerous way to allow our kids to think, both literally and figuratively. So many societal problems have surfaced in the last two decades that we can no longer afford to ignore the effects of allowing our kids to be self-centered. As society's outlook on behavior changes and adapts to what we now consider normal behavior, it may be too late to effectively restore normal and respectable behavior in our society.

Even as the behavior of Americans deteriorates we see other countries, which emulate western society, facing their own behavioral problems in their own societies. Japan, once a monument to proper, respectable, traditional behavior, is now dealing with some of the same behavioral issues we have grown accustomed to here in America. The manners and traditional rituals that once distinguished the Japanese culture as noble and proper are falling by the wayside as Japanese youth are behaving like their spoiled American counterparts.

I hate to be redundant about parent's lack of responsibility when it comes to raising kids these days, but if behavior is learned, parents are doing a miserable job of teaching.

Although poor parenting is a large part of the behavioral breakdown, mom and dad are not the only reason our children are learning bad behavior. Anybody familiar with cable television can get a good idea of why our kids are going astray and where our society is heading. Even in the few locations where cable is not available, there's always satellite television or a few network channels. Television has pushed the envelope to the point we've become tolerant (or maybe numb) to a constant bombardment of language, sex, violence and generally disrespectful behavior. Even on stations designated "Family" channels or "Childrens" stations there is a proliferation of inappropriate language and subject matter. I'm no prude and enjoy some of the programming I'm describing. I'm also an adult who has choices and knows how to exercise them. Our children, on the other hand, are being told their watching family channels and kids networks while being subject to some very risqué content.

Last week while flipping through the channels I paused on The Family Channel, a cable station formatted around family friendly programming (or so the name implies). Within the few minutes I watched the show (that happened to be on at 6:45 pm,) I saw one Black female (talking into the camera) about another black female who was in the background. She referred to her as a "Hoe," three times. She also referred to this "Hoe's" boyfriend as a "Stupid Negro." The only reason the word nigger wasn't used in this case is because it *was* The Family Channel. Now I think we all know that the word "Hoe" on the streets refers to a slut, a whore, or a prostitute. "Stupid Negro" is about the most derogatory and racist thing I've heard on prime-time cable in a while. Is it any wonder when our kids watch family programming and learn to speak like this, that we're appalled when we overhear a conversation between adolescents at the mall?

Violence and sexual situations are more common on prime-time television today than ever before. Our kids don't shutter or even blink when a bad guy gets shot in the head or blush when they see a man having sex with two women. Homosexual situations are becoming commonplace and soon the gay agenda will have accomplished its goal of making homosexual situations normal to our youth. No longer will seeing two guys French kissing on screen give kids that "Icky" feeling inside. As sexual content becomes more explicit and violence becomes more gruesome, kids become more desensitized. Is it any wonder we hear of pre-teens having sex and babies or Junior high school kids going on shooting sprees? We reap what we sow, and so far we've planted the seeds of violence and deviant behavior in our kids minds. Until the stimulus they're constantly exposed to changes, we can expect to see an increasing amount of ghastly and appalling behavior from our sons and daughters. We can blame the programs on T.V. or we can get smart and change the channel. It is, after all, our job as parents to supervise what our kids do and watch and participate in and who they hang around with...Remember?

Doing things that intentionally hurt or belittle others is what kids do for fun now. Watching the kids in our neighborhood, that are my sons age, has made me glad I exercised my right as a parent to choose who my son associates and hangs out with.

Our neighbor's children, who are between ten and fourteen years old, can be heard over the fence on any given summer day cursing like sailors (often at the parents) when asked to do their chores or help around the house. The first summer we lived in our house this behavior just about floored my wife and I. Jaw dropping is a good way to describe the reaction to hearing these kids talk the way they do. I also noticed they behaved like dogs left alone too long, when their parents were gone. Every time the kids were outside they entertained themselves by destroying something. Sometimes it was beating on their small above ground swimming pool with a baseball bat, sometimes it was starting fires under the wooded swing set. Regardless of what they did, their behavior was destructive.

Other kids in the same basic age group (ten to about fifteen or sixteen) act with the same disrespect for adults and each other. Groups of kids frequently walk down the middle of our neighborhood streets and don't pay any attention to cars trying to drive on the roads. These kids simply refuse to get out of the way until the last second and then look pissed off at the driver for making them move. Sometimes they won't move out of the way until the driver honks, then they flip off the driver or throw things at the car. To me, this is shocking behavior. It's also not tolerated by myself and three or four other people on my block. To everybody else it's "Just the way kids are." I've heard grown adults say, "They're kids, that's what kids do." Not my kid! Not any kid that doesn't expect to receive a good ass whoopin' from his folks or from the driver of the car he just threw a rock at. We've called the police about the matter and have been told that unless they catch the kids in the act of refusing to yield to cars, there's nothing they can do. Even if caught in the act these arrogant punks know there's not much a cop can do but tell them to use the sidewalks. Even towards the police, these suburban kids show no respect and have no fear of getting into trouble.

As a generation of rude and disrespectful kids have grown, and now have children of their own, the societal norms of respect for ones elders, respect and reverence for the law, and common courtesy towards ones peers have all but disappeared.

Youth today have little or nothing to do with our nation's elderly. In fact, instead of associating with our seniors by volunteering at senior centers and nursing homes and learning from their stories and experiences, our kids park in their disabled parking places and poke fun at their slow pace. Not too many kids will hold a door open for our elderly citizens, nor will they offer to assist an older neighbor with household chores or yard work. All the common courtesy things I used to do as a kid to help out an elderly person having difficulty have been ignored for so long they've been all but forgotten. We've really let our kids down by not promoting the contact between them and our nation's seniors. The life lessons and traditions that have been lost as a result of this generational disconnect cannot be restored. The sad thing is that our kids will never realize what they've missed because they can't miss something they've never known.

Poor treatment of their elders is repulsive enough, but we're now seeing a new and more defiant generation of young punks who have absolutely no admiration, respect or reverence for America's law enforcement. There are pre-teens and teenagers on our streets today that literally laugh (if not spit) in the face of authority. Again, as a kid I always had the utmost respect for our town's policemen and sheriff's deputies. When I saw them I would say, "Hello." I'd ask about what was going on in our small town and I always wanted to show them I was a good kid who followed the rules and stayed out of trouble.

Too many of today's ill behaved youth pride themselves on challenging the law instead of abiding by it. These youngsters seem to get a sense of pride from having run-ins with the police. Respect is gained among today's kids not by how well you play a sport or how well you do in school, but by how far you're willing to push the boundaries of poor behavior. Braggadocio comes from telling your friends about how you sassed the cop who arrested you for shoplifting or breaking and entering. Pride comes from telling others all the bad things you've done without getting caught.

Rude behavior isn't just kids pulling pranks anymore. Rude behavior has escalated into the commissions of violence and crimes. Murder among teenagers is a direct result of the way our kids treat one another. Rude behavior has opened the door to more than poor table manners or the total lack of chivalry in today's society. Rude behavior has opened a nation's eyes to the horrors created when people treat each other with total disrespect and with an utter lack of courtesy.

With societal behavior declining and the threat of severe punishment for crimes no longer a deterrent, is it any wonder our youth are finding it easier to behave poorly? Too many thumb their nose at authority, whose hands are largely tied when it comes to enforcing laws not to mention morality or ethics. According to figures from the U.S. Department of Health and Human Services (www.aspe.hhs.gov), the youth violent crime rate has increased dramatically and steadily in the past thirty years. Violent crime, defined as murder, forcible rape, robbery and aggravated assault, has increased from 58 incidents per 100,000 persons under 18 years of age in 1965, to 231 incidents per 100,000 in 1994. That is roughly a three hundred percent increase in teenage violent crime over the course of thirty years. According to the same source, violent crime statistics for the 12-year-old age group were not even significant enough to report until 1980 and have since risen each year. The figures also show that males commit violent crimes at a higher rate than females but it's alarming (at least to me) that female adolescents between the ages of twelve and eighteen have been committing violent crimes at a steadily increasing rate year after year since 1985.

Accordingly, youth homicide rates have been on the rise since 1970. Although the murder rates between races differ drastically the fact that these numbers have been so consistent in their increases is reason for concern.

The homicide rate, committed by minors of all races, rose from 8.1 murders per 100,000 in 1970 to 20.3 murders per 100,000 in 1994. While the rate for white minors grew each year, the rate for black youths was shocking. In 1970 there were about 65 murders per 100,000 committed by blacks ages 15-19. By 1994 that rate had risen to almost 136 per 100,000 among the same demographic. That's nearly a 210% increase over the course of less than twenty-five years. Cultural factors and differences can be cited for the lopsided proportion of violence among minorities, but the bottom line is violent crimes committed by teenagers of all races are on the rise.

What all these facts and figures allude to is the value of human life and the respect shown to others has been on the decline among our nations youth for more than thirty years.

Our kids are rude and as they continue to grow even ruder, we'll see the violent crime and murder rates soar. In fact the lack of common courtesy and dignified treatment of their peers has bred a new phenomenon among teenagers in our nation's schools.

School shootings were nearly non-existent before the 1990's. As our kids became ruder to one another and began treating each other with more ridicule, hazing and physical abuse, some teens that couldn't handle anymore poor treatment from their peers snapped. It was big news when Eric Harris and Dylan Klebold killed classmates and then themselves at Columbine High School in Littleton, Colorado. The country was shocked when Kip Kinkle killed his parents and then opened fire on his classmates at a high school in Springfield, Oregon. It really started in Grayson, Kentucky in 1993 When Scott Pennington (17 years old) shot and killed his English teacher and a janitor. From there, shootings at schools have grown common and range from incidents in Alaska to New York, Washington and Oregon to Minnesota and from Maryland to California. No town, large or small, is exempt from the possibility of a school shooting. Wherever there are bullies tormenting underclassmen and wherever there are kids being picked on by their peers, there is an atmosphere conducive to violence.

In fact, the national news media acts appalled and shocked when reporting on each of a rash of school shootings. These events have been occurring more frequently over the past decade. The sensationalism and media attention given to these events further the likelihood of similar events occurring again. These stories of violence beg the question, "Why did we let things get this far?" There have always been bullies and there have always been kids who have been picked on. Now, unlike times gone by, bullies are far more cruel, demeaning and violent. And now, unlike times gone by, those being picked on are finding immediate and permanent ways to stop their tormentors.

In nearly all of the school shootings that have taken place in the past decade, the root cause of the violence was a direct result of how the shooter had been treated by his peers. Being rude and mean is all the rage but it can also get you shot by the very person you focus your insults and ridicule on.

It's all about behavior and about the way we treat our peers and counterparts in society. We teach our kids by example. By setting a good example of how to treat others, our kids will emulate and eventually learn to treat others well. Likewise, if parents treat others poorly in front of their kids, the youngsters will emulate and eventually learn to treat others in this fashion. Unfortunately, parents have been setting bad examples too often and for too long and now our society is reaping the results of examples sown by rude and irresponsible parents. As time goes on and these kids have kids, the behavior becomes more and more appalling.

It's not just each other that youngsters and teens treat poorly; it's also the property of others. Vandals have always been a pain in society's neck, but today's vandals (largely pre-teens and teenagers) perform more acts of vandalism and more severe vandalistic acts than ever before. According to a report by the U.S. Department of Justice (www.ncjrs.gov) the number of juvenile vandalism cases increased 48% between 1988 and 1997. I believe this shocking increase is a direct result of the lack of parenting going on in a majority of households during this time frame. It directly reflects the time when computers became prevalent in American households and when video games had started to replace the imagination and the physical activities that used to keep kids busy. By 1988 most two-parent households saw both parents working. Those employed by companies involved with the technology boom spent far more time at work than with their families. Demand for the new technology required employees to work more hours. This gave kids more unsupervised free time after school and weekends to get into trouble. As the frequency of vandalism increased so did the severity of the crimes. No longer where our little hoodlums tossing rocks through the windows of abandon buildings and spray-painting railroad cars. The new breed of vandals is breaking and entering to do damage inside businesses and buildings and setting fire to residences and structures that often have occupants inside. As society continues to grow ruder, the severity of the crimes committed by our rude youth is increasing.

Kids have little respect for their own belongings because few have to work to earn them. Why would they have any respect for other people's belongings? If destroying the property of others is done in such nonchalant manner and if the severity of the vandalism continues to escalate, how do we reverse the trend? One idea is to make the punishment for the crime severe enough that kids think twice about committing them. In fact, I think the example of the American teen in Singapore being caned for vandalism was a good one. It would serve our spoiled American youth well to receive and acknowledge corporal punishment for senseless acts of property destruction. This, of course, would never happen. The A.C.L.U. simply won't stand for the just punishment of criminals in our society, regardless of the offender's age. They'd rather give these youngsters a proverbial (never literal) slap on the wrist and turn them loose to commit bigger and better crimes, as they get older. Without any real repercussion for crimes committed by teens, it's difficult to deter kids from continuing their pattern of criminal behavior.

People have become self centered and that applies double for the majority of our nation's children. Parents spoil their children as a form of guilt for not spending time with them and for not performing the duties of a parent. When little Bobby wants a new bike or a video game, mom and dad jump up and run to the store to buy it. This is how too many parents show their love. Buying whatever it is their kids want, instead of teaching their kids what they need to know, is a poor child raising strategy. One result of this form of "Child rearing" is that the kid becomes expectant of whatever it is he or she wants. "It must be gotten for me and it must be gotten now" is the attitude of many youngsters today. Life revolves around their plans, desires and immediate needs. Kids have no concept of what's going on around them when they are so focused on their own self-gratification. Anybody in his or her way will be ignored, cursed, assaulted, or killed. They see this as acceptable behavior because they've been allowed to think that obtaining their desired object takes priority over all else. I honestly don't know if our kids intend to be rude or if they simply have no idea of what proper behavior is. It frightens the hell out of me to think that our kids have no concept of manners, integrity, or even right and wrong anymore. Our youth are starting with a foundation that's seriously dysfunctional. What do we have to look forward to as they bring the next generation into the world?

We either adjust our outlook on politeness, accept that kids are rude, that school shootings "Just happen," and learn to adapt to an ever-increasing violence rate *or* we could start teaching our kids some manners.

There doesn't seem to be much of a decision to make for me. Unfortunately, I feel that I'm in the minority when it comes to holding our kids to higher standards. Too much time has passed since parents demanded politeness and manners from their children. As a result, today's parents simply don't know that they *should* be teaching their kids to respect their elders, to say "Please" and "Thank you," to treat others as they'd like to be treated, to respect authority, to develop proper table manners, and to use appropriate language.

I hope it's not too late to change the way our kids act and behave. It saddens me to see what our society has come to regarding the rudeness and callousness displayed by our young children and teenagers. Unfortunately, I hold little hope that the behavior of our youth will change for the better. Too much has been lost and too little attention is paid to the behavior and manners of our kids. At best, we can hope that the behavior displayed by the youth of our society doesn't deteriorate any further, but this is probably an optimistic wish. Parents who grow up being self-centered and utterly rude simply lack the ability to teach their kids to behave the way kids *should* behave.

Our kids are rude! Go against the socially accepted tide and give the extra effort needed to be sure *your* kids are polite and treat others with dignity and respect.

# CHAPTER 10
# THE ENVIRONMENT IS FINE!

Ted Danson, known for his portrayal of Sam Malone in the 1980's sitcom Cheers, predicted in the late '80's that the world's oceans would be dead within ten years. Luckily for you and I, Mr. Danson is better trained as an actor than an oceanographer.

There are a plethora of Hollywood actors and actresses who have jumped on board the Wacko left's green machine. Environmentalists welcome the well-known faces who lend themselves to the extremist cause. These folks may well be able to entertain us, but they have a total lack of knowledge concerning the well being of Earth's environment. Sure, they receive all the normal talking points that are drilled into the heads of all environ-whacko's, but they have little or no concept of the real world outside of their Hollywood bubble.

The claims of global warming are true. The fact that the ice caps are melting and that global temperatures are rising is no surprise to anybody with even a vague understanding of our planet's history of warming and cooling cycles. But being masters of the obvious, environ-whackos point out these natural phenomena and then (as all self-hating Liberals do) they shift the blame of these events to human influences. It amazes me how incredibly dim-witted these self proclaimed "Nature experts" are. It seems awful poppas to me that these folks actually believe that humans are significant enough to have such a tremendous influence on a planet that has been through 4.5 billion years of *actual* earth-changing events.

It's absurd that environmentalists cite internal combustion engines, used only for the last hundred years, for the increase of greenhouse gases in our atmosphere. The effect of the "Pollution" produced by our consumption of fossil fuels is infinitesimal compared to a handful of the biggest volcanic explosions on record. The fact that volcanoes have been erupting for billions of years in varying severity all over the planet is of little interest to the environ-whackos. The millions of tons of ash, rock, gas and other debris sent into the atmosphere following a violent volcanic eruption dwarfs any other singular pollution- producing event in the world. Wouldn't it go to reason then, that natural occurrences and events are the reason for the climate changes throughout history? Warming and cooling trends have been occurring since the formation of the planet. Yet Greenies would have us believe that my Chevy Tahoe is the sole reason for the rise in the ocean's temperature. They claim my gas-guzzling S.U.V. is the cause of the extinction of animals in the rain forest resulting from rising global temperatures. How cruel and insensitive of me.

Of course we know that the miniscule, if even scientifically detectible, effect humans have had on the earth's overall well being is simply not significant enough to actually change global temperatures in the slightest. Greenies tell us it's not only humans that pollute, but also those things humans require to sustain life such as food, transportation, shelter, etc. Let's look at one of the more entertaining claims made by Greenies. They claim that the cattle we raise for food and dairy products have significantly raised the amount of green house gases by releasing "Dangerous" amounts of methane into the atmosphere. The only real danger of this methane gas would be if you were somehow caught behind a bovine while it was in the process of releasing the gas. That's right! The environ-whackos blame cattle farts for melting ice caps. The only reason cattle are demonized by Greenies is because humans eat cattle and therefore must have over-bred the food source to the point of damaging our atmosphere. Apparently, *only* animals bred for the survival of humans emit ozone-destroying gases. I've never heard the Greenies blame Wildebeest or a roaming herd of Elk for the destruction of our environment. Have they also proven that the dinosaurs that roamed the earth for 65 million years were of a fart-free breed?

I find it hard to believe that Greenies could convince anybody that the "Damage" caused to the earth by humans would have any substantial or actual effects on the global environment. Still, automakers are spending billions in R&D to devise environmentally friendly cars. Low-emission vehicles are nothing more than the politically correct response to a screaming bunch of self-loathing environ-whackos.

To look at the effect of gasoline consumption on the environment we should look at the history and evolution of our planet. If we use a clock as a comparison we can see how little time humans have been here and how extremely miniscule a time pollution-causing machinery has been in existence. If twenty-four hours represents earth's history, and midnight represents right now (or as far as the earth has come thus far) then humans arrived and evolved into Homo Sapiens at only 17 minutes 'til midnight. Therefore, machines like the internal combustion engine and factories that create pollutants have been in existence for a few fractions of a second. How can it be claimed that pollutants that have been in existence for less than a blink of an eye could be responsible for the environmental trends Greenies are attempting to blame on humans? How very self- important they must believe themselves to be in order to claim responsibility for the changing global conditions.

I'm waiting for the environ-whackos to realize how much polluting debris is created in a volcanic eruption.

During the 1980 eruption of Mt. Saint Helens, more than 1,200 vertical feet of the mountain was blown to bits. Prior to the eruption the mountain stood 9,760 feet above sea level. Following the blast the elevation was knocked down to 8,525 feet. Ash columns rose to fifty thousand feet and ash clouds dropped ash and acidic debris over thousands of square miles of protected forestlands.

Isn't it a shame that the environmentalists were unable to stop the eruption of this incredibly politically incorrect mountain? Think about it! Thousands of trees were slaughtered before any injunctions could be sought by greenie groups from Liberal activist judges to stop the eruption. This means that the nesting areas for countless species of birds were also destroyed, inevitably injuring or killing helpless eggs and chicks in this violent and utterly unnecessary blast. The forest floor, which had been home to an abundant variety of wildlife, was turned to liquid mud as the snow and ice melted and the pyroclastic flow engulfed everything in its path. Rivers, streams and lakes that provided an ecosystem for numerous species of fish and amphibians were obliterated before any protests could be organized. (Although I'd have like to seen a huge group of environ-whacko protestors convene on the mountain when it blew...just to see if they'd made any difference.)

These are only a few of the direct and immediate effects of this relatively small blast. Eruptions tens and thousands of time the size of Mount St. Helen's have been happening on a regular basis around the globe for billions of years. They will continue to happen regardless of the Greenies hate for sources of pollution. No amount of protests or demonstrations can deter a volcano from erupting, and no extremist judge can impose an injunction to halt future eruptions, pending environmental impact studies. Yet we hear very little from the Left regarding the pollution created by Mother Nature while demonstrating her normal and expected behavior. Why is that? Could it be that through the eyes of confused environ-whackos, the gases, ash, pollutants and devastation produced by Mother Nature is not to be considered pollution since it's "Natural?" Is it the way these "Byproducts" are released into the atmosphere that makes the difference between whether they're categorized as pollutants or non-pollutants through the eyes of our not-so-bright Greenie friends? I think so. Sort of like the difference between those damn cow farts and the natural gaseous emissions released by a heard of beautiful wild elk.

It would stand to reason then, that oil, natural gas and coal (all natural products) found within the crust of the earth would be considered non-polluting as well, right? Those products might well be listed as acceptable in the eyes of the Left, except for the fact that humans have found a way to benefit from them. As a result, any product that can benefit mankind must be demonized and condemned as dangerous to us, both as a nation and a species. Their self-loathing attitude won't allow

Liberals to accept that the benefits of fossil fuels and other natural resources far outweigh the miniscule pollution created as a byproduct of their use. Here is some of the rather over-simplified "Reasoning" displayed by our self-proclaimed intelligent environmentalist nuts. Gases expelled from volcano…Good! Gases expelled from gas engine…Bad! Gases expelled from volcano… not pollutants. Gases expelled from engines…bad pollutants.

It is just ridiculous to assume humans are influential enough to have any substantial impact on our climate. Yes, the planet is warming. Yes, it will continue to warm. Yes, the sun is getting hotter and will continue to do so for several billion years to come. Yes, ice caps will melt and sea levels will rise. Yes, species unable to adapt to the subtle changes in climate will become extinct. These are natural and historical cycles that have occurred over billions of years and will continue to occur long after humans have become extinct.

Another ridiculous assumption made by environ-whackos is that cutting timber for our nation's growing needs is a bad thing. If you listen to the Greenies speaking at rallies and gatherings in Portland, Chicago, New York or Los Angeles, our country is on the verge of destroying its forests and killing all the species wildlife that call the forests home. Most of these freaky folks are throwbacks from the '60's and '70's or a new breed of environmentalists being bred in our liberal-run colleges and universities. The old nuts are as whacko and off centered as ever, but the new breed has evolved into a more desperate, more violent breed of extremists. Both groups preach the gloom and doom playbook that depicts Americans as greedy cruel and uncaring when it comes to utilizing our severely depleted forests for human gain. They'll have us believe trees are on the verge of extinction and as soon as we finish cutting them all down the earth will die… or something like that. To be honest with you, I never pay these yo-yo's any attention because I know the facts. Here are a few for you to throw out at a Greenie the next time he/she opens their uneducated mouth.

According to The *Bugwood Network* (**www.bugwood. org**) the United States has 2,263,259,000 total acres of land area. One third or roughly 737,000,000 acres are classified as forestlands. Ten percent of that forestland are National Forests. Fifty-nine percent is categorized as "Private non-industrial" land. Seventeen percent is public non-national forestland. An unbelievably small amount of our nations forestland is owned by the evil timber industry. Just 14% of the nations forestland is timber-industry owned. How can it be that we've killed nearly every tree in the country when eighty-six percent of the nation's timber is virtually untouched? The same source reports that the total forest area is still nearly seventy percent of what it was in 1600. More trees are growing in our nation's forests today than were growing in 1900 and total growth per acre has increased 71% since 1952.

As the facts show, our nation's trees are treated like the important natural resources they are. Reforestation has led to healthy and plentiful forests. In fact over-forestation is more problematic now than at any other time in our nation's history. As a combination of replanting and then being denied the ability to cut timber in many regions, our forests are becoming overpopulated by the trees the enviro-nuts are trying to save. This leads to thick underbrush that supplies abundant fuel in the event of a wildfire. In the mind of an environmentalist, the idea of thinning timber to promote healthy forests is just a ploy used by the evil timber industry to get their greedy little hands on more trees.

In the end, the ignorance of these Greenies cause intense and widespread forest fires that destroy far more timber than is harvested each year by the logging industry. Even following catastrophic fires, the environmentalist lobby to block the salvage of standing or fallen dead timber. This makes even less sense than trying to ban the cutting of live timber. Why let a perfectly good resource go to waste after it has been killed in a wildfire? It's simple. Greenies are adamant about humans not being able to benefit from the resources provided by Mother Nature. In no way, shape or form are humans allowed to exploit nature for their own personal use. Forget the fact that these hypocrites live in houses built of wood, use paper and cardboard in their making of protest signs, and wipe their holier-than-thou little butts with toilet paper.

Our forests are more dense than they have been in 100 years and our reforestation policy is the best in the world. It only makes sense to utilize our nation's timber for the thousands of uses for which timber is needed. Why pay astronomical prices for imported lumber from Canada or Russia when we could be utilizing our own abundant supply of wood? By doing so, we could put thousands of former timber workers back to work by re-instituting jobs that have been systematically eliminated by timber regulations and environmental lobbyists. Rural communities that once thrived in the Pacific Northwest and in the Northern East could benefit greatly from the rebirth of the timber industry. Schools, towns and entire regions could once again thrive.

So let's say it like it is! Liberals who whine about the economy and cry about the unemployment rate are literally blocking the ability for America to reinstate hundreds of thousands of jobs and generate huge amounts of revenue for rural communities and states. We must fight for the lifting of timber cutting bans, the abolition of roadless areas and demand common sense be put back into the policy making process as related to our forests.

Just as ridiculous as the current timber cutting restrictions, are the restrictions on domestic oil drilling. Liberals whine about the ever-increasing gas prices and the effect it has on the poor folks in America. Liberals, as we all know, are the voice of compassion for the poor and downtrodden in our country, and are very quick to point out the "Barriers" that hinder the happy lives deserved by the unmotivated in our society. Gas prices obviously gouge the poor more than the rich and have a more adverse effect on the lower-income folks in our society. Therefore, it would go to reason that Liberals would be in favor of doing whatever was necessary to lower gas costs for these poor folks, right? You bet. Make more oil accessible and thus lower the cost per gallon for fuel. The theory is simple and makes sense…and that's why Liberals fight it tooth and nail. That, and the fact that Greenies believe that drilling for oil would destroy our pristine earth. Oh, don't get me wrong, drilling in South America or Iran has no ill effect on the planet in the minds of the environ-whackos, it's just domestic drilling that would bring certain Armageddon.

NIMBY or Not In My Back Yard is a motto of the Left. Ted Kennedy touts the importance of alternate energy, but blocks energy companies from building wind farms off the East coast where he resides. His views may be obstructed and the construction may inconvenience him. Maybe the possibility of actually solving a problem he's been bitching about for years, is just unthinkable. Whatever the reason, bitching about the problem is to be expected. Also to be expected is the bitching from Liberals when a suggestion is made to solve the problem. So it goes with Oil drilling in America's back yard. Whether it's ANWR in Alaska, Texas, Wyoming or off America's coastline, environmentalists fight adamantly to ban domestic oil drilling.

Their argument is that the process of drilling will severely disrupt the flora and fauna of the environment in which it's being done. Therefore, we simply can't drill regardless of the repercussions of being almost totally reliant on foreign oil. Again with oil, as is the case with pollution and timber, the main reason drilling is demonized is because these environmental extremists simply can't justify harvesting natural resources from Mother Earth to benefit man. Oil is natural. Oil is vital to our society. Oil is abundant in numerous places under American soil. Yet a minority of extremists are holding it hostage to the rest of us by implementing bans on drilling and refining. Liberal judges rule to ban based on their personal opposition to oil drilling and not the laws regarding the issue. Thus, we are handcuffed and forced to rely on other nations for the oil we use to maintain and advance our society.

A few extreme environmentalists may truly believe that drilling will cause irreparable damage to our planet, but I'm convinced most Liberals opposed to drilling have ulterior motives. Oil makes the world go 'round. If America has readily accessible stockpiles of oil, it will continue to be the most powerful nation in the world. That in itself should inspire any self-respecting Liberal to shut down domestic production. As self-loathing residents of our country, Liberals would like nothing more than to see a strong and independent America become dependent and reliant on other nations for the oil that fuels (no pun intended) our national economy.

Our environment is fine. It's infinitely stronger and more resilient than liberal environmentalists will ever give it credit for. Earth has been here long before humans arrived on the scene and will continue to thrive long after we depart. There is little we could do in the routine of our sorry little inconsequential every-day lives to inflict any measurable or lasting damage to such a huge and intricate planet. Global warming is real. So is global cooling. These are cycles that have occurred for millennia. This phenomenon is *not* the result of human pollution, regardless of what the Greenies tell you. It's natural and will continue to happen for millennia to come.

It's a pretty arrogant and misguided flea that believes he controls the actions and behavior of the dog on which he lives.

# CHAPTER 11
## TERRORISTS ARE BAD!

Terrorists are bad! There, I said it. They are not misunderstood. They are not courageous. They are not noble, religious warriors. They are killers and bad people. When will our enlightened Liberals in Washington realize this? How many brutal murders and attacks on innocent civilians around the world will it take for Liberals to open their eyes and realize that these folks despise the United States and "Infidels" around the globe?

Following the atrocities of the 9-11 attacks, Americans stood united and committed to bring to justice those responsible for the deaths of three thousand of our fellow Americans. Well that lasted about five minutes. It wasn't long at all before Liberals started to forget about the attacks and began making excuses for those responsible for bringing down the World Trade Center and damaging the Pentagon. Not only have we removed responsibility from the terrorists, we actually placed the blame for the attacks on the *victims*. I guess

Liberals figured it worked well in our criminal justice system to take responsibility off the criminal and transfer it to the victim, so why not apply it to matters of terrorism and national security?

It really shouldn't surprise us that intellectual types like Colorado's Ward Churchill and other "Educators" around the country would applaud the actions of the terrorists while demeaning the character of our president. After all, these folks blame America and Americans for all the world's problems. We're damn capitalist pigs who deserve everything we get from extremists around the world. According to the "Hate America" Liberals, terrorists kill in the name of religion; therefore it's not only justified, but noble. They take that reasoning one step further and demonize our president and military for retaliating against those wishing to do us harm. It simply isn't right that the big bad U.S. sends trained killers into other countries to destroy the infrastructure that produces terrorists.

It would be poetic justice if one day the biased mainstream media had to report a story about one of these Liberal idiots whose family had just been killed in a terrorist attack. I bet they'd change their opinion of terrorists then. You can be damn sure they wouldn't be blaming their family members for getting themselves murdered. In fact the idiot would probably be asking, "Why?"…"After all the support I've shown and excuses I've made for these indiscriminate killers, why did they go and kill *my* family?" These guys simply don't understand that terrorists don't care who they kill. In the name of Allah, they're justified in killing everyone. Put that in your liberal pipe and smoke it Mr. Churchill, Mr. Kennedy, Mr. Kerry, Mrs. Feinstein, Mrs. Boxer and the rest of the "Hate America" liberal legislators in our nation's capital.

Liberals don't stop at blaming the victims of terror and glorifying the terrorists, oh no. They take it a step further by actively searching for "Violations" in the treatment of captured, captive terrorists. Unlike their counterparts in the war on terror, U.S. Soldiers aren't allowed to torture and then behead their prisoners. Actually, they're not allowed to do much more than provide food and shelter for them, all the time making sure the prisoners are not offended or intimidated.

"Atrocities" at Abu Graib prison in Iraq were front-page news for months. Pictures of naked prisoners and vicious dogs showed the world how evil and callous American G.I.'s were. This was fantastic for the "Hate America" crowd. It showed that Americans couldn't be trusted to detain enemy prisoners and that American soldiers were more brutal than the terrorists who after all, are just fighting to protect their way of life. What kind of evil acts did our soldiers perpetrate on these misunderstood, noble and courageous terrorists? Well apparently we stripped these guys naked and made them pose in sexually suggestive positions. We also allowed our guard dogs to intimidate the prisoners by letting them bark at the terrorists. Some of these neglected detainees were even forced to wear underwear on their head...underwear on their head! Can you believe that? Awful!

Never mind that terrorists had been raping, torturing and cutting the heads off of Americans. These folks were kidnapped while working for companies intent on fixing and developing the Iraqi infrastructure and brutally murdered. It amazes me that the Liberals in this country can turn a blind eye to the atrocities carried out against their own countrymen and at the same time make a case for criminal charges to be brought against the guards at Abu Graib.

It can't be made any more obvious that Liberals are on the side of America's enemy. These traitors anxiously awaited the American death toll to reach 1,000, and then 2,000 as the war in Iraq progressed. Their celebrations were masked as protests, but make no mistake, they hope and pray for the enemy to win. This means that American soldiers will die in what Liberals see as an unjust war. Just like we deserved to be attacked on 9-11, our soldiers deserve to be killed because they're perpetrating atrocities on the terrorists, the insurgents, prisoners and Iraqi civilians. We simply don't belong in Iraq. Even if being there is imperative to preventing future terror attacks on American soil.

During the mess Americans have come to know as "Election season," 2004 presidential candidate (and Vietnam War veteran) John F. Kerry told the American people that we should be "Fighting sensitive battles" in Iraq. What the hell is a sensitive battle? Should we be shooting Styrofoam bullets out of rubber band guns so as not to injure the enemy? Should we require our soldiers to throw water balloons instead of fragmentation grenades?

Perhaps we could call ahead our plans to raid weapon storage facilities and give the enemy time to evacuate the arms being used to kill our soldiers. That would be very considerate. It would be a nice gesture to ground our fighter planes and attack helicopters as well. It's just not fair that we have all that firepower and the enemy doesn't. How these sensitive battles would lead America to victory in Iraq is unclear to me. Then again, I'm just a stupid working-class Conservative and Mr. Kerry probably doesn't *expect* me to understand his intellectually superior strategy for winning the war on terror. Far be it for me to assume that wars are won by killing the enemy and destroying the infrastructure the enemy relies on. We learned in Viet Nam that a war fought from Washington couldn't be won. Mr. Kerry, of all people, should understand that our military has to crush the enemy with as much force and speed as possible to limit casualties inflicted on our troops. It puzzles me why he and his elitist Liberal buddies in Washington, are doing all they can to take the rifles out the hands of our soldiers and the strategic plans and decision making abilities away from our generals in Iraq. Actually it's simple; they want us to lose the war in Iraq and show the nation what a poor leader

George Bush and the Republicans are. Like everything else in Washington, Liberals consider the war on terror and our national security nothing more than political leverage issues.

Does it make any sense that charges are brought against guards at Guantanamo Bay where terrorist suspects are held? It may sound cruel and insensitive, but the treatment of these terrorist murderers is of little concern to me. As far as I'm concerned, we're wasting time and manpower by keeping them incarcerated in the first place. Kill them and be rid of the threat they pose to our country and its citizens. It's that simple. They have proven their intentions are to kill any and all Americans if given the chance, so why do we coddle them? They're allowed to worship. We're made to supply them with their religious materials. They're allowed to be represented by lawyers. We're forced to provide representation for these killers. They complain of torture during interrogations. We do internal investigations and punish the interrogators who are trying to elicit information vital to our national security. Does any of this seem asinine to anyone else?

Perhaps we should supply them with seventy virgins since we've taken their right to kill themselves in a suicide bombing away. If they could detonate themselves in a crowd of Americas they can go to heaven and do whatever it is they do with these young gals. It would only make sense then to supply them with these young tarts since we've denied them the right to "Earn" them on their own. I'm sure if it were actually suggested, our Liberal leaders would fight for this right to be granted to those poor incarcerated "Alleged" terror suspects.

Appeasement is the plan and peace is the goal. Liberals fail to realize appeasement doesn't work and peace simply isn't possible in a society that panders to terrorists. Bad guys must be gotten rid of before the good guys can develop a peaceful and prosperous society. Maybe we should send our Liberal leaders back to the third grade until they can understand simple concepts and institute at least *a little* common sense among the members of the Democrat Party. How are these dimwitted individuals finding their way into positions of power in the first place? Are there that many Liberal Americans in this country? If so, we are in deep doo-doo. Liberals simply can't be trusted with the security of our nation or the responsibility of leadership.

If those who despise America are put in charge of leading America, what are we to expect but the destruction of America? It's time we enlighten our Liberal intellectuals and force them to realize that the terrorists, and not Americans, are the bad guys. We must refuse to allow their distorted views of America to influence policy in our great nation. I'd also like to see some of our more prominent Liberal leaders like Teddy Kennedy and Barbara Boxer brought up on charges of treason and publicly hanged like we did to traitors in America not so long ago. It would be a great reminder that there are boundaries to the harm you can do to America.

The media should be held accountable for the information they report to the American public. In the eyes of our Liberal policy makers, the "Big three" and mainstream media in general, have had a wonderfully negative affect on the public perception of the war. Run by Liberals, the news has reported on 100% of the tragedies befallen upon U.S. troops, the loss of innocent life as a result of the war and the negative effect the war has had on every aspect of life in Iraq. Never do we hear about the positive things being done for the people of Iraq. The schools that have been built, the torture chambers and assassination rooms that have been destroyed, the lives saved by removing an evil dictator from power, the rapes that have been prevented, the institution of a democracy, the freedom granted to citizens of all socio-economic classes and the improved general living conditions, are just a few of the things the mainstream media absolutely refuses to report.

Any information that sheds a positive light on the results we're seeing from our efforts in Iraq must be buried or ignored. Anything that proves the Bush administration was justified in entering into a preemptive conflict must be discredited. Interviews with soldiers that are happy to be fighting the war on terror and helping a nation find its freedom will not be aired. Yet interviews with a disgruntled vet, critical of the war, are plastered all over the newspapers and T.V. screens for days on end. Cindy Sheehan receives endless media attention while the parents of other troop lost in battle, who still support the war effort, are shunned and ignored. The media no longer cares that it's obviously and deliberately biased. The arrogant executives at ABC, NBC and CBS filter and pre-digest the information they want us to hear. It's a blatent attempt to influence public opinion and support. Never mind that the information on your T.V. screen every night is lop-sided and often incorrect.

Like Liberal leaders in Washington, Liberals in the media hope for, and actually take an active role in, the failure of our efforts in Iraq and against the war on terror. What is good for the betterment of the country is bad for Liberals. Thus, good things must be undermined. Conservatives must be demonized as warmongers and occupiers of nations. Bush must be attacked personally and repeatedly and proved to be bellicose and incompetent. This has been pounded into our heads since the war began and can still be seen every night on the evening news.

It seldom matters to the press that they perpetuate misinformation and often report half-truths or outright lies. The bottom line is to undermine the administration and turn public opinion against the war. The media takes a soft line on "Human interest" stories that tell of how terrorists are misunderstood. They take the time and effort to research and explain the terrorist's outlook and the reasons for killing innocent bystanders in an effort to please Allah. These stories are "Vital to understanding the enemy," we're told by some smug, self-important guy in a suit when we flip on the television. Personally I don't want to "Understand" the enemy. I want the enemy dead. You want to give me a story? Report to me why Liberals hate their country and hope with all their might for it's defeat. I'd be interested in uncovering that little mystery. Report why Liberals remain American citizens since they despise America. Explain what would happen if they moved to another country and bad-mouthed it as they have done here in the United States. What's that? There's severe punishment and even death for those who undermine and subvert the government of many foreign nations? Wow! Guess they've got it pretty good here in the land of the free…that they despise so much.

Many Americans truly appreciate the FOX News Network for its more balanced and centered reporting. It's about the only news network on which I've heard any stories of inspiration from Iraq. FOX reports about the I.E.D.'s and the coalition troop casualties same as the big three do, but they don't report *only* about the negative aspects of the war. They continually have stories if inspiration as related to the building of schools and the repair and expansion of the Iraqi infrastructure. They actually talk to the soldiers and their commanders and when they do, we hear proud American's who are honored and glad to be part of such an important war.

They're optimistic and tell of the accomplishments they've achieved. FOX puts a face to what the big three only refers to as, "U.S. Troops."

The shows aired on FOX News Network are not afraid to report the truth about shocking or appalling incidents and aren't afraid to honestly and truthfully give the whole story without adding this, or excluding that, to slant the perception of the story. There are no excuses made for criminals, terrorists, or any other bad guys. In interviews there is always sympathy for the victim and the blame is placed squarely on the criminal. It's refreshing to get real, factual news and not some diluted or exaggerated interpretation of it. Keep leading by example FOX.

We must never forget that the terrorists are the enemy. Regardless of what our Liberal political geniuses or the arrogant news media would have you believe, terrorists want to kill westerners and especially Americans. Their goal is the total destruction of western society. The chaos that would follow would truly be the beginning of the end for civilized nations around the globe. Apparently many of America's elected politicians would like to see the same thing. They defend the actions and "Rights" of those who do us harm and bash those who stand up to the perpetrators of terrorist acts. Then they claim to be every bit as patriotic as you and I. How is giving aid and comfort to the enemy and promoting legislation that makes America vulnerable to future terrorist attacks, being patriotic? I'd like to have old Teddy or Hillary explain that one to me.

These same folks claim to oppose the war but support our troops. Newsflash… Our troops are the ones fighting the war you oppose. How can you support one without believing in the other? Tell the truth and say what you really think of our military men. This is what I gather the Left believes to be true about our men and women in uniform:

- All enlisted military personnel, while having noble intentions of serving our country, are largely uneducated and are generally simple folks.

- Military leaders are power hungry brutes with no compassion or tolerance for other cultures or ideas.

- The military is the enforcement arm of the Republican right, and the Right's agenda is to conquer the resources and political influence of all nations.

- The military is unfairly strong and too well trained to be put on the battlefield against lesser forces, from weaker nations, which will incur severe casualties, should battle take place.

- All military personnel are bloodthirsty killers who have been given a gun and a license to murder.

- The military is largely unnecessary to a nation as civilized as ours. Peace would prevail if only the ignorant Republicans would realize our military is the reason for (and not the solution to) armed conflict around the world. Get rid of the American military…get rid of global tensions. It's that simple.

That's how these patriotic, troop-supporting Liberals really feel about our brave men and women in uniform. Liberals have short memories. They neglect to acknowledge that without the military superiority America has developed during the course of our history, we would not be the nation we are today. Of course this fact would surely please most of the Liberals working so hard to deconstruct our nation. But without the sacrifices of our fathers and grandfathers, Liberals wouldn't even have the chance to unite to destroy what our elders fought and died far. Anybody sense a little irony here?

It's important to know who the bad guys are. Most bad guys come from other nations and despise the prosperity and freedom that America has fought so hard to achieve. But some come from within our country and within our own government. They're called Liberals and they're more dangerous than plastic explosives strapped to Muhammad. They work from the inside to help make America vulnerable and so far they've accomplished too much. Their hate for our society and our way of life is obvious and it is flagrantly displayed each time a Liberal politician votes to pass legislation protecting terror suspects, or restrict the military from obtaining intelligence that can save American lives.

Our self-proclaimed "Enlightened" Liberals blame America and console the misunderstood enemy. They sponsor and support legislation that makes America vulnerable while tying the hands of the administration and military striving to make our nation safe.

Let's get together and tell these idiots that America is the good guy. Terrorists are the bad guys. We will not tolerate your pandering and compassionate attitude towards people who kill our fellow countrymen. We will hold you accountable for your actions and votes in Washington. We're tired of you blaming America for the world's problems and will no longer tolerate your slander. Perhaps we could even try these buffoons on charges of treason. Liberals, wake up or shut up. Period!

# CHAPTER 12
# ILLEGAL ALIENS ARE
# JUST THAT...ILLEGAL!

W e're all immigrants or descendants there of. Our ancestors traveled to the new world to escape persecution or to make a new start. They were some of the first immigrants to America. As the years past, America became know as both the "Land of opportunity," and the "Melding pot of the world." The opportunity to live in such a great and unique country has generated a diverse mix of immigrants from hundreds of countries throughout the world. This is what has made America a great country and has lead to its unprecedented success in an unbelievably short amount of time. In the past, immigrants were eager to become legal citizens of the United States. They applied for citizenship and studied to pass the test that would allow them to become full-fledged American citizens.

Unfortunately for all those who've worked to become legal citizens, there are many immigrants who enter the country illegally. The reasons for being in America have changed as well. Not everybody enters the country to better their lifestyle, to find a job, or even to establish a stable home for their family. Some unscrupulous immigrants bring with them the drug trade, crime, gang activity, and the very real threat of terrorism.

The topic of illegal immigration is a hot-button issue right now and will continue to be a topic of animated debate for the foreseeable future. It's also a point of contention between President Bush and conservative Republicans, myself included. As a president who adamantly strives and fights for national security it surprises me how lax Mr. Bush is on controlling our nation's borders. Our border with Mexico is severely undermanned and is the major point of entry for illegals into the United States. Most may come with good intentions, some don't. Regardless, they are here illegally. That means they are criminals living in America without permission and should therefore be sent back to their country of origin.

Those critical of the Bush administration have placed the blame of illegal immigration solely and squarely on the shoulders of Mr. Bush. History, even recent history, tells a different story. Although I feel Bush has taken a soft approach to the issue, statistics from 1990-2000 show Liberal icon Bill Clinton allowed his share of illegals into America during his tenure in office. Before Clinton, Reagan granted a "One-time" amnesty for illegal aliens as a way to allow those already here, to stay and to put and end to future illegal immigrants gaining access to America. No, it didn't work then and it won't work now. On paper, amnesty looks like a good way to accept our losses and prevent future problems. In actuality it simply gives illegals more of a reason to get to America in hopes of being here when the next amnesty is granted.

In fact, thousands of "Anchor babies" are born in the U.S. each month. These are children born in America to illegal aliens. Once the children are born on American soil, they are "Entitled" to all things legal citizens are entitled to. This includes education, healthcare and social services. It makes no difference that the parents of these newborn Americans were here illegally at the time they gave birth. Where is the down side of sneaking across the border to give birth? There is little or no deterrent in the form of punishment for those who get caught. Even if returned to Mexico, there is absolutely nothing to keep them from attempting to sneak back into the U.S. the very next day. Drop a baby in the states and receive free money and services from the American government. Things need to change!

There are countless ways illegal aliens negatively impact our nation. These folks (who we supposedly have to count on to keep the wheels of capitalism turning) should be as unwelcome as they are uninvited. It really doesn't matter how hard a person works if they are working illegally. Why is this so difficult for Liberals to understand? Our government should enforce laws already on the books by prosecuting those who provide jobs or services to illegal aliens. Is there a difference between providing food and shelter to an illegal alien and providing food and shelter to any other criminal? Hell no! The term "Aiding and abetting" should be used to describe the actions of those who provide aid to illegal aliens. Government agencies, food banks, businesses that employ illegals and counties and states that refuse to identify and deport illegal aliens, should be prosecuted to the fullest extent of the law. Those marching and protesting for rights that allow illegals to enter, and remain in, America should be brought up on charges as well. They are openly and unapologetically providing aid to criminals who create numerous problems in our society. Once upon a time, folks who offered aid and comfort to those who did our nation harm were once referred to as "Traitors." Now they're called advocates and are fighting for the rights of criminals entering our country illegally. We must begin to Identefy and deport illegals. We must also identify those who aid illegals and punish them. Tighter borders and a lack of benefits and privileges, as well as a lack of jobs for illegal aliens might just be enough to keep them in their own country. Our national identity is on the line here. Without action, much of America will become "Little Mexico." Lets look at some of the issues we face as a result of illegal aliens.

## EDUCATION:

It may sound a bit rough, but I'm plain sick and tired of hearing about the numerous social problems being created to benefit illegal aliens. Our public schools (already nearly worthless) are suffering as a result of Hispanic children that don't speak English. My child learns less because special attention must be paid to little Juan who is learning English as a second language. I'm not prejudice and actually speak Spanish myself, but if foreign kids can't keep up, send them to specialized ESL classes (billed to taxpayers, of course) until they're able to understand the curriculum being taught in America's schools. Better yet, if they're in the country illegally, they should be sent back to whatever nation they came from. Let them attend school there.

It's asinine and dangerous to lower educational standards for American kids so that non-English speaking children can meet the new and reduced requirements. This effectively cheats America's youth out of any quality education.

The expense to American taxpayers to educate non-English speaking children is astronomical. The price tag will only increase as we continue to grant educational rights to, "Anchor babies." There seems to be an urgent effort to educate foreigners at any cost while at the same time trying to generate enough revenue to support schools that "Educate" American kids. Every day I hear stories of budget cuts to our nations elementary and high schools. It's too bad for those kids who have programs cut, classes overcrowded and teachers who are too overwhelmed to provide quality instruction. Yet, in a show of compassion and political correctness, Liberals find abundant funding for Head Start programs and specialized classes for those who don't yet speak English. Is it any wonder our educational system continues to graduate functionally illiterate kids?

## CRIME:

The violence from gangs that have migrated north from Central and South America, as well as Mexico, is being felt across the entire nation. It's an issue that no longer affects just Miami or Los Angeles; it has seeped into the Pacific Northwest, the Midwest heartland of America, into the Southern states and up into the Northeast. These aren't groups of people who come to America to pursue the American dream, they come here to manipulate and prey on a naive society. Their level of violence is shocking. The most notorious of these gangs is MS-13. Their members are young, tough, street-smart punks who have little regard for the lives of anybody outside of their gang. They beat, torture and kill to establish dominance in drug trafficking. They sell "Protection" to retailers and street vendors in urban areas by extorting up to half of the proprietor's weekly earnings. These folks are opportunistic vultures who we've allowed to enter our country. They violate and abuse America's businesses, children and citizens. Murder rates in cities infested with Latino gangs are on the rise. A spike in violent crimes, sex crimes, prostitution and racketeering are evident in areas saturated with gang members in America illegally.

The Violent Crimes Institute recently concluded a study, which reveals some shocking statistics related to crimes committed by illegal aliens. During a twelve-month study, the Violent Crimes Institute found that illegal aliens who committed serial rape, serial murder, sexual homicide and child molestation were present in 36 of our nation's states. In other words, 72% of our states harbor violent criminals and sexual offenders here illegally. And that numbers only reflects *convicted* illegals. Violent crimes committed by illegals are no longer a problem that affect only border-states. The same study shows that there are approximately 240,000 illegal immigrant sex offenders currently in the United States. That works out to about 93 sex offenders illegally entering the U.S each day. Most shocking to me was the fact that 63% of the illegal violent criminals and sex offenders had been previously deported for other offenses, prior to being convicted for murder, rape or molestation.

Our border policy is frightfully inadequate when criminals, already kicked out of our country for committing crimes, are allowed back in only to commit more heinous crimes. The victims of these violent illegal aliens are largely U.S. citizens. Seventy percent of the victims of illegals are citizens of the United States, while 30% of victims are fellow illegal immigrants. When we allow criminals to cross the border into our country illegally, we are inviting and encouraging violence and crime. The Violent Crimes Institute concluded that, "The U.S. faces a dangerous threat from sex predators who cross the U.S. border illegally." (For additional statistics and findings from VCI research please visit: (www.diggersrealm.com)

The last time I checked murder, rape and child molestation were still unacceptable in our society. Liberals are promoting change and soon even these most hideous of crimes may just become more acceptable in America.

## Economy:

Many illegal aliens work in the agricultural industry making small wages at "Under-the-table" jobs. Most pay no taxes to help with the infrastructure of the country they've invaded and in most cases they send a large portion of their earnings south of the border, not even stimulating local economies. They take jobs that many feel should be assigned to able-bodied individuals currently living off the welfare system. I'd rather see a "Recipient" *earning* his benefits than pay illegal aliens good money to do the same job. The economic effects on a nation invaded by illegal aliens are as obvious as they are numerous. In depth studies have been done concerning this issue but I only find it necessary to point out here what should be obvious. Wages are kept low as a result of an over-abundant workforce. Funny how Liberals promote a "Living wage," yet they can't grasp the concept that illegal aliens drive wages down. At the same time they demand living wages, our kind-hearted and compassionate Liberals are demanding relaxed laws regarding illegal workers. Another example of Liberals attempting to institute policy that would contradict their stated goals. If it is the wish of Americans to weaken our economy and to promote the hiring of cheap illegal help, then keep supporting the Liberals and their America-destroying agenda. Our financial security is a great place to begin the undermining and eroding of our nation's foundation.

## NATIONAL SECURITY:

Larger and more important yet is the real and current threat of terrorism occurring on American soil. It *will* happen again, it's just a matter of time. By allowing open passage from Mexico into America, we're inviting terrorists into our nation with open arms. There are too few Border Patrol agents with too little authority to deter illegal aliens from entering America, and far too many miles of border to patrol. How difficult would it be for Akmed to dress like a Mexican farm worker and zip right into the very country he wishes to desroy?

It's most likely already happened. The issue of border security simply doesn't seem to concern our government. What will the reaction be when the next terrorist who attacks on American soil says, " I met no resistance crossing the Mexican border, where I entered Arizona. From there I traveled to Chicago where I blew up all those people in the sports stadium?" Terrorists must be laughing at the ease they are able to enter the very country they brutally attacked just a few years ago. Who can blame them for laughing?

It seems obvious to me that illegal aliens are a huge problem. Does anybody else see the inherent problems with our government's current stance on illegal immigrants? Illegals serve in our military...Hello! They vote for America's leaders...Hello! They receive benefits intended to assist needy Americans...Hello! They are granted free medical care at hospitals ...Hello! What needs to be done to wake up our slumbering leaders in Washington and make them confront a problem that could become the ruin of our country? Unfortunately, the politicians in our nation's capital are more concerned about votes, about not offending anybody and about coming across as understanding and compassionate. Liberals main concerns are *not* protecting American citizens and upholding American Law.

Immigrants a century and two centuries ago came to America to find wok and create opportunities they simply didn't have in their native country. This created a strong commerce and business atmosphere with a strong workforce. Unlike immigrants in the past, too many of today's illegal aliens come to America not to find opportunity and to support themselves, but to obtain benefits from our government. They receive welfare, food stamps, legal advice, medical care, housing assistance and a hundred other things without having to do a damn thing for them. Today's immigrants are working hard to develop and adopt the entitlement mentality that is so common among Americans. Unfortunately our government is not only allowing this to happen, they continue to support those illegally in this country. This will only serve to invite more illegals into America to enjoy what their respective countries won't provide for their own citizens.

Also unlike immigrants from years gone by, today's immigrants (especially illegals) don't come to America to become part of America. They come to America to form small versions of the country they just left. Little China, little Mexico, or little Russia exist in the suburbs of any number of American cities. These folks seldom associate with anyone outside of their ethnicity. They don't assimilate into the "American" population. They segregate and isolate themselves to form their own communities, separate and apart from other nationalities. They're not Americans, just Mexicans, Laotians, or Indians, living in America. They utilize and take advantage of all America has to offer without contributing a damn thing back to American society. They exist much as a leech does, sucking off its host and offering no benefit in return. Yet we're to respect and admire their cultures and religions and beliefs, but there's no reciprocity when it comes to them respecting our culture. They demand all the rights granted to Americans and even advocate for special rights since they're "Minorities," while at the same time the rights of Americans are being infringed upon. How does any of this better our nation?

Unfortunately there are groups here in America that don't see the danger in continuing to allow illegal aliens into the country. They have no comprehension of sovereignty and believe that illegals should (and do) receive the same rights afforded to American citizens. In their politically correct attempt to nominalize the seriousness of the immigration problem and to soften the rhetoric surrounding immigrants here against the law, these advocates have developed new and less offensive terms for illegal aliens.

We are now all too familiar with terms like "Undocumented" Americans, "Visiting" immigrants, and "Guest workers." These phrases are intended and implemented to make illegals feel more welcomed and Americans less offended by those commiting the crime of entering America illegally. The advocates for these illegal aliens are the same folks who take responsibility away from criminals and make excuses for their actions. They attempt to grant all the rights enjoyed by American citizens to any and all who can run, walk, swim or fly across the border. Never mind that until one gains citizenship legally, he/she should not be extended the rights of American citizens. Advocates fight for health care for illegals. They provide legal council for illegals. They advocate for government paid housing for illegals. Why not just sign over the country and let a group of immigrants, here against the law, who speak little or no English, run the nation? In essence, that's what these advocates for illegal immigrants would like to see happen.

In fact, The United states government actually forces social service workers and private service providers to aid and abet criminals. Illegal aliens are criminals by definition. To knowingly provide food and shelter to a criminal is against the law. The laws we have in place to stop illegal immigrants from gaining access to our country are ignored. The laws that tell us we can be punished for aiding and abetting a criminal are on the books, yet our own government forces service providers to deliberately break the law by providing services and benefits to illegal aliens. It's confusing, isn't it? It's a *fact*, that by giving illegal aliens food stamps, free or subsidized housing or even food boxes at the local church, crimes are being blatantly and repeatedly committed. Government regulations prohibit volunteers at food pantries to even *ask* the immigration status of recipients. The good-natured folks who volunteer at these pantries are forbidden to ask legal status and are therefore forced to provide service to clients both legal and illegal. This makes the volunteers criminals. The good-hearted souls handing out food to the hungry are breaking United States law by aiding and abetting criminals. The government ought to be called on this one. Forcing individuals and agencies to provide equal service to legal and non-legal individuals is criminal in and of itself. This practice should not be tolerated, let alone mandated!

Here it is. Illegal aliens are in this country illegally. They've violated U.S. law by entering America. They pose a threat to our national security. They are granted billions of dollars worth of government services that they should not be entitled to. They hinder the learning process of American kids in our public schools and they segregate themselves into small communities that have no benefit to American culture.

Our government has ignored the problem for decades and continues to turn a blind eye to a very real threat to America. Amnesty only serves to promote more illegal immigration. Deportation may be costly, but by looking at the cost to allow these folks to stay in America, it's the only real option that would insure a long-term solution to an ongoing problem. We've got to give our Border Patrol agents the authority to effectively close the borders and utilize the means to actually deter illegals from crossing it. Our government needs to sanction or otherwise punish the Mexican government for actively promoting the migration of illegal immigrants from Mexico to the U.S.

Enough is enough! Common sense tells us that illegal aliens are bad for America. This is why the Liberals love them. This is why we need to put an end to the problem before it's simply too late to take action. Keep America safe for Americans and for those willing to immigrate to America in an orderly and legal fashion. Enough said!

## Chapter 13
# Bad Behavior Isn't Normal

No matter how hard progressive society tries to convince me that I'm wrong or old fashioned, I don't stand for bad behavior. It's wrong and it should not be tolerated. Instead of addressing some of the nations biggest problems by enforcing good behavior among our youth and young adults, our society promotes poor and even dangerous behavior. Teen pregnancy, drug use, homosexuality, bad language, poor English, a lack of respect for others and a hundred other issues confronting our society are promoted, instead of denounced, in our national media.

We already know our kids are rude. We discussed that earlier. What we need to acknowledge is that poor behavior is the sole reason for our kids being so rude. It's a shame that our society has decided that broadcasting shows instructing young viewers how to behave poorly, is acceptable and entertaining. We see it with the constant and relentless bombardment of homosexuals on "Do-it-yourself" shows and the promiscuous teens on any number of prime time TV shows directed at the teen audience. We see it with the excessive and graphic violence in movies rated "R" and more and more in movies with a rating of "PG-13." The language, too, is just as appalling. Video games also teach our kids and young adults how to act. Got a problem with somebody? Beat the hell out of them or just kill them. It works in the video games, doesn't it?

Normalizing and promoting behavior that is rude, unacceptable or downright appalling is not a good idea. This social experiment will produce nothing good in our society. Still, our entertainment industry promotes teenage sex, drug normalization, if not downright legalization, the use of violence to solve differences and a blatant disregard for manners and respect for others. Strange then, isn't it, when our kids end up pregnant, drug addicted, violent and totally disrespectful? Go figure.

Inattentive parents, who overlook or ignore the fact that all these movies and shows and games are having a detrimental effect on their kids, are part of the problem. When these kids begin to act like their mentors on prime time television or on the big screen, parents wonder, "What the heck got into little Johnny to make him act like that?" Bad behavior isn't anything a responsible parent and or adult would teach a kid, is it? If so, we're in it deeper than I thought. Actually we've become systematically numbed to bad behavior. Like a dentist rubbing novacane on our gums, the media has been desensitizing us as to what we perceive as normal and acceptable behavior.

What was once expected as the norm for behavior has gone out the window. Now there are few expectations and no norms. By "Celebrating diversity" we've erased "Normal" and instituted chaos as related to societal behavior. We've been taught that "Being different" should be celebrated and not frowned upon. That goes just so far before it becomes a justification for bad behavior. If little Johnny is in the school cafeteria and bites into what he thinks is a chicken nugget, but turns out to be a fish stick, how should he react? Should he quietly discard the fish stick into a napkin, pocket it and go on with the other selections on his lunch tray? Sounds reasonable to me. But today it's just as acceptable to spit the fish stick across the room, throw your lunch tray across the cafeteria and scream your distain for fish sticks. Teachers may still frown on this behavior, but would surely allow it because they've been trained by child psychologists to recognize that little Johnny is just expressing himself. Poor behavior is okay if you truly mean it. Is that the message we want to continue teaching our kids?

There seems to be a lack of control among kids today. They throw more tantrums, they strike their parents, they demand and expect more than ever. Is it just a coincidence that the demand for ADD drugs has shot through the roof in the past two decades? Every kid who acts up or throws a tantrum is labeled as hyperactive or diagnosed with one disorder or another. We're putting our kids on potentially dangerous drugs instead of teaching them proper behavior in the first place. What we need to do is swat them on the ass when they misbehave.

Our modern behavior modification experts have decided that a "Time-out" is the best thing for a kid. They also tell us to ignore tantrums by allowing a child to scream and carry on until the child gets tired. Since the time when a slap or a swat was deemed cruel and politically incorrect, these new child-rearing methods have proven their worthlessness and foolishness time and time again. We've been conditioned to raise our kids in a way that has been proven to fail. Oversensitive parents who coddle their little bundles of joy are doing them no favors and are unintentionally paving the way for the kids to grow up to be demanding and misbehaved. When a disciplinary approach to child rearing was commonplace our society was much more polite and far better behaved. Seems to me if this approach has worked for centuries it would continue to work if we allow it to. I can't understand why some ninny-nanny child behavioral "Expert" would want to hinder success and promote failure when it comes to our kid's behavior. This is one social experiment that has had a dramatic and long-lasting affect on our society. The social engineers behind this little experiment have done such a good job of blurring the line between acceptable and unacceptable behavior that the last couple of generations truly don't know the difference.

I'm certainly not advocating for beating your children every time they step out of line, but I do support common sense when it come to raising our kids. A good disciplinarian seldom has to slap a hand or swat a butt because a well-behaved child can usually be "Reprimanded" or "Straightened out" with a stern look or word. If a child knows there are repercussions for misbehaving, he or she is less likely to misbehave. Simple, ain't it?

The simple fact that mom or dad is *willing* to smack your ass is usually enough deterrent to keep a child on his or her best behavior. Strange that it always seems to be the parents of the worst behaved kids who are appalled at the thought of physically disciplining a child.

In this strange and alternate-universe-like state we now refer to as reality, parents are submissive wimps who allow their kids to rule the roost. If you actually act like an adult and a responsible parent you're viewed as mean. Insensitive and barbaric are words used to describe parents who teach and expect manners and respect from their children. It's gone so far that the idea that, at adult gatherings, children are to be, "Seen and not heard," now borders on child abuse. Instituting chores and having kids actually do something for their "Allowance" is frowned upon. Setting curfews and bedtimes is unfairly restrictive. House rules and expectations are antiquated and obsolete. Again, is it any wonder our kids come out the way they do? We must expect more from the parents if we are to see any improvement in the general behavior and attitude of our youth. This fact seems obvious and simple to me yet there continues to be studies and debates as to how best raise our kids. Parents simply have to take control, instill manners and morals, hold high standards, teach by example and be stern when necessary.

Unfortunately, Liberals and intellectual academic types have taken child-rearing tools away from parents. The result of blurring the line between acceptable and unacceptable behavior can be seen on any given public school campus in the country. From Pre-schoolers to high school seniors, child behavior in our country is shocking and shameful. Well-behaved kids are today's equivalent of "Nerds" and the old school "Bad boy" classification pretty much covers the other 90% of the kids in school.

In fact, two middle school girls in a school less than 100 miles from my house were convicted of attempted murder last year for dumping rat poison into a classmate's milk carton. A grade school boy was caught carrying a gun on a local school bus. Certain restriction on clothing such as trench coats or excessively baggy jackets must be enforced at our local high schools to eliminate the possibility of kids smuggling weapons into class. In all the local junior high and high schools boys must be reminded to pull their pants up so as not to reveal their butt cracks and girls must be reminded to wear enough clothes to cover their breasts and nether regions. Do these strike you as kids who know the difference between acceptable and unacceptable behavior? It's a good example of the old adage, "You reap what you sow."

It may just be too late to expect parents in the future to reverse this trend by teaching their kids what acceptable behavior is. The fact is that these parents-to-be will have been raised in times when knowing the difference between right and wrong and acceptable and unacceptable simply weren't important. Therefore they'll have no idea what to teach their kids, more less *how* to teach them. This is where we are. Is this where the Liberals intended for us to be? All indications point to, "Yes."

## CHAPTER 14
# WE'RE TIRED OF THE GAY STUFF

It's not just me. It's every single one of the people that I've talked to about it. We're all sick and tired of flipping through the channels and seeing the gratuitous homosexual on nearly every station. It ain't right and it ain't normal!

In an effort to normalize the homosexual lifestyle, Liberals and their friends in the media are pushing the gay agenda. As a society, America is saturated with references to homosexuals, their lifestyles and the issues relating to gays. Since the late 1980's homosexuals have been pouring out of the proverbial closet in shocking numbers. They are more boisterous, flamboyant, prominent and annoying than they've ever been before. Thanks to cable and satellite television Americans have access to hundreds of television channels. Thanks to the gay agenda , Americans can't enjoy those hundreds of channels without having to put up with homosexual oriented shows, programming and networks. Lets take a look at the "Gay thing."

First I'd like to state I'm not a so-called "Homophobe." I don't dislike homosexuals any more than I dislike criminals, liars, cheats or any other group of people I deem morally reprehensible. Since I've never been referred to as a "Criminaophobe," or a "Cheatophobe,"I don't consider myself a "Homophobe." In fact, the word "Homophobe" itself was designed to be a label attached to anyone and everyone who doesn't wholeheartedly agree with the behavior and issues facing gays and lesbians. Call me what you will, but I still oppose homosexuality on a moral and societal level.

In the past several years we've seen the introduction of gay characters into prime-time programming. Sitcoms like Will and Grace, Movies of The Week, home improvement shows and feature films all began sneaking a gay character in the mix of main characters, usually as the butt of a joke or an oddball character. Soon the gay character had significant roles and now the entire shows are designed around the lives of gay characters. By slowly introducing and then normalizing homosexual characters and behavior, the media has opened the door to forcing the gay lifestyle on us, with little or no resistance, because we've become desensitized to the concept. When I see two men holding hands and kissing I feel ill in the pit of my stomach. When teens today see the same thing, they simply recognize the fellows as a homosexual couple. That is shocking and appalling. The difference in outlook between my generation and my son's generation reflects the incredible and dangerous influence the media has on our society.

This normalization has been well planned and well executed. It has effectively taken a taboo subject, (better left in the seedy shadows of our society) and brought it out in the open for all to see and discuss. Gay issues, gay rights, gay marriage, gay adoption, gay, gay, gay. It seems to be all I hear anymore. Society has opened a crack in the moral door of our nation and homosexuals have been pouring through it ever since. In fact the door has been slowly pried and pushed and now stands wide open, exposing the majority of moral Americans to the "Plight" of the gays. Gay issues affect a miniscule percentage of American citizens. Gay groups and gay activists would have us believe that these issues are important and should be given credible consideration. I'm sorry, but when a lesbian couple goes to court to get one of their names put on the birth certificate under "Mother" and the other under either "Father" or "Partner," your wasting my tax dollars. The kid is either adopted or conceived out of that homosexual relationship. Therefore, two women should not be allowed to claim mother and father rights (unless procreation has changed drastically since my last college biology class) for a child.

Gays getting married is as ridiculous to me, as them having kids. It's a sad day in America when we must spell out the obvious…marriage is between one man and one woman. Period! How far have we slipped when cases for two men or two women, to be legally married, actually find their way into court and are given serious consideration by our judicial system? Pretty damn far, I'd say. It sounds ridiculous, but we're just getting started with corrupting the traditional family and traditional relationships. In an ever progressing "Do it if it feels good" society, traditional beliefs and morals are falling to a movement that strives to justify and normalize a variety of unacceptable behaviors.

By flipping to any number of design or home improvement shows on cable television we are assaulted by what I now refer to as "The gratuitous queer" on nearly every program. He's usually the one working with curtains and fabric glue instead of power tools and hammers. Most are overly flamboyant and strut around the set acting like…well…like queers. They talk with a lisp, go crazy over fabric and color choices for any given project and generally make me want to turn the channel. Why can't TLC or Discovery air programs where men do men things and women do women things and drop the homosexual sexual innuendoes put forth by a guy doing girl stuff? The last thing I want to hear while trying to get ideas for landscaping my backyard is some gay guy lisping about how he and his "Partner" just put in a romantic patio swing. Save it! I don't want to hear about it. In fact I'm changing the channel…only to be assaulted by more gays on the next show. I resent the "All gay-all day" programming being aired on what seems to be an "All queer-all year" network. We are given little choice but to suffer through homosexual indoctrination if we wish to watch these otherwise informational and entertaining shows.

Then we have Hollywood creating a movie billed as "A beautiful love story." The only hitch is that it's about queer cowboys. Brokeback Mountain (or as I call it, "Bare-Ass Mountain") is nothing more than another attempt to normalize homosexual behavior. Their logic is that if two cowboys (icons of the American west and a symbol of strength and toughness around the globe) can be shown as sensitive and caring homosexuals, then homosexuality really *is* okay. I'm sure we're not far away from movies portraying the president of the United States as a homosexual. Maybe he and his "Partner" will fly around in Air Force One touting the importance of gay acceptance. He'll pass legislation that is homosexual-friendly and promote programs beneficial to gays. The movie will serve to implant the idea of a caring gay man as president and portray the benefits to gays if a gay man was ever elected president. It then won't be long until a gay man decides to actually run for the presidency and, thanks to the success of the movie, will be viewed as a legitimate contender in the race for president. See how easy it is to normalize immoral behavior? Just show a lot of people or important people engaging it and then suddenly...presto... it isn't so bad. This sends a very dangerous message to our youth.

Our kids are currently so unaware of right and wrong that they don't even know that they *should* know the difference. If normalizing homosexuality is pursued long and hard (no pun intended) enough, our kids or our kid's kids wont even know the behavior is immoral and repugnant. And that's precisely their goal! It will no longer be shocking when Bill and Lance are kissing in the movie theatre or Suzan and Amy are holding hands while shopping in the mall. That's just what they do. No different than John and Lisa making out, right?

How about the business of gays adopting babies? We've all heard how loving and motherly Rosie O'Donnell or Melissa Etheridge are and how they and their "Partners" offer a loving and nurturing environment for "Their" children. Come on! Am I to believe that our nations adoption agencies actually believe that a gay household is a safe and suitable environment for a child to be raised? What brain surgeon is in charge of the adoption agency? That person should be committed to a nut house! With thousands of heterosexual (see normal) couples, experiencing fertilization issues willing and eager to adopt, why place a vulnerable and influential infant or child in a house of moral decay?

What kind of sick person would subject a child to the mental and emotional turmoil of being raised in a house where two men or two women are having sex in the next room? It's completely asinine. Yet it happens across America. Slap a child for misbehaving or spank a kid for screwing up and Child Protective Services will take your kids away and label you as an abusive parent. It's these same idiots who then turn around and give a child to a homosexual couple. Punishment for wrongdoing = Bad…Submitting a child to immoral homosexual behavior = Good. Does this make sense to anybody with half a brain? Maybe I'm just not enlightened enough to understand the situation.

Can you imagine little Johnny at his first Little League game with his mommies in the stand cheering him on and hugging each other when he gets a base hit? How about Jimmy's daddies showing up to videotape his Christmas pageant at school? It makes for a very uncomfortable situation. Instead of the "Parents" staying home, or at least not attending the events as a "Couple," they demand equal treatment. Equal treatment is granted to equal people. Homosexuals are not equal to heterosexuals. They're different. If they decide to act differently than mainstream society then they ought to expect they'll be treated differently, too. After all, we don't treat child molesters the same as non-molesters, criminals the same as non-criminals, dishonest people the same as honest people, so why is it we're expected to treat immoral sexual deviants the same as "Normal" folks? I will not conform and bend my tolerances because somebody who acts and behaves in an immoral fashion feels offended when they're treated "Differently." That doesn't make me a bad person, quite the opposite. It shows folks that some people are still willing to adhere to their beliefs, stick to their morality and stand against corrupting influences in our society. In other words it makes me a bigoted, prejudiced, closed-minded homophobe. At least that's what the progressive Liberals call me.

Now these deviants are on the offensive. Those of us who enjoy a traditional heterosexual marriage and covet traditional family values, are now being labeled for doing so. The latest name that gays and lesbians have attached to heterosexuals is, "Breeders." These freaks are actually attempting to give a negative connotation to those who conceive children in the conventional (and only physiologically natural) way, humanly possible. Also, the gay folks are so proud to apply for "Same-sex- marriage licenses," that they want to pass that joy on to the rest of us. It's been proposed, in states more tolerant of the idea of gay marriage, that heterosexual couple should be forced to apply for an, "Opposite-sex marriage license." No longer is a marriage license an acceptable term because it's not sexual-preference-specific. This boggles the mind!

Like other negative influences in our society, homosexuality has been introduced and has since been increasing in prominence in the media. Like the violent and graphic video games and movies that desensitized kids to violence and the promotion of sexual activity among teens (that has lead to the increase in teen pregnancy rates and boosted the spread of S.T.D.'s) normalizing homosexuality will have its negative effects on our kids. The result will be a no-big-deal attitude toward immoral behavior in general, and a specific acceptance of the behaviors displayed by gays and lesbians. Same-sex "Experimenting" will then become more frequent among our youth because the moral stigma of having sex with a person of the same gender will have been erased. With this will come more cases of sexually transmitted diseases including a spike in the spread of AIDS. So eventually, normalizing homosexuality will bring death and disease to our kids. Does normalizing homosexuality sound like a politically correct cause you'd be willing to promote? Me neither.

So let's send a message to Hollywood and the television networks that insist on promoting, even celebrating, homosexuality. Refuse to watch that home improvement show that features Lance making valances. Be sure to boycott the movie that degrades American icons by portraying them as queers. Teach your kids that same-sex relationships are not normal and they're not right. Refuse to be indoctrinated into the acceptance of immoral and unethical lifestyles. Go to school board meetings and investigate the curriculum being taught in "Acceptance" and "Tolerance" classes.

We've seen how special interest groups respond when they're acknowledged. Instead of keeping a low profile and working quietly to benefit their interests, they stage huge parades and find the most public stage to force their lifestyles or beliefs on the rest of America.

Gay rights, gay-day parades, gay-pride marches, gay nights at theme parks and a hundred other gay-oriented events are examples of how small groups of people are screaming for attention and acceptance. And they've received it. Homosexuals cannot be turned away for jobs, services, or any other benefits formerly issued to heterosexual couples, families or individuals. It's illegal to discriminate against an individual on a sexual orientation basis. That translates to…."We the government are forcing you to accept homosexuality because if you don't, you'll be sued and slandered into oblivion." We can no longer display or even voice our disapproval of the gay lifestyle, or those who participate in homosexual activities, without legal action being taken against us. To stand up for moral behavior and denounce immorality ensures we wear the label of prejudiced and bigoted.

Of course our celebrities are in on the act, too. Not just portraying gays in motion pictures and weekly sitcoms, but advocating for gays in public service announcements and at organized rallies. Because "Alternate" lifestyles are more accepted in Hollywood and New York than they are in Omaha or Fargo, celebrities use the cities as a venue for their advocacy. Elton John is recognized as *the* spokesman for AIDS and contests that he wants to make folks aware of the disease. He's lost dozens of close friends and colleagues to the disease. He and other singers and actors solicit funds from the government and the private sector to "Address the issue of AIDS." They complain that our government isn't spending enough to find a cure or vaccine and that America should be ashamed of itself for the way it's handled the AIDS epidemic thus far. The problem is that Elton John is openly gay. He flaunts his flamboyancy and sings songs celebrating diversity and acceptance. Never do I hear these celebrities denouncing the homosexual lifestyle that has been a major contributor, domestically, in the spread of AIDS since the early 1980's. Maybe next we'll see Keith Richards bitching about his health problems and asking for more medical research into his numerous health conditions without denouncing the use of illicit drugs and acknowledging the cumulative effects they've had on his body over the decades. The point is that these do-gooders are complaining about the effects of a disease while refusing to address one of the main causes for its prevalence. Why bitch about spilled milk if you're not willing to put the cap back on the jug?

Another aspect of the "Gay thing" rears its ugly head where it's needed the absolute least. Bubba Clinton was the genius behind the "Don't ask, don't tell" military policy. This is so absolutely preposterous that *only* a Democrat could institute this policy. Homosexual soldiers can now serve in the United States military if they don't reveal that they're gay. It's amazing how the government looks at gays when it comes to national defense as opposed to national entertainment or employment. It's okay to acknowledge there are negative issues surrounding homosexuality in the military, but the government refuses to acknowledge that the same issues surround civilians in every-day life.

Why can't employers institute a strict don' ask, don't tell policy in the office when a gay employee makes his or her co-workers feel uncomfortable? Because if homosexuals felt they couldn't express themselves and be proud of their sexuality, they would sue (and win) on the basis of discrimination. Why can't we blackball gay actors in Hollywood who portray their deviate lifestyles in movies and TV shows seen by our kids? Because this would offend homosexuals and they would sue (and win) on the basis of discrimination. So why then, is it acceptable to tell a soldier, "Keep your mouth shut if you're gay?" Shouldn't they too be allowed to express their sexual preference? It seems awful discriminatory to me that their civilian counterparts are allowed to celebrate their gayness while a gay soldier is silenced and forced to internalize his or her gayness. What kind of crude, insensitive and intolerant military is our government running? That this is even a topic of discussion in our society is disgusting and ridiculous. Soldiers are men and women of honor; gays are not. Soldiers fight wars; gays fight for homosexual rights. Soldiers defend our nation; gays are corrupting our nation. Soldiers believe in the rights of Americans; gay distort and abuse the rights insured by America.

Why would homosexuals, who have little in common with our soldiers, want to become a military person and defend a country they largely despise? Some say, "Homosexual soldiers are just as patriotic and capable of fighting as anyone else." That may be so, but who wants to be stuck in the middle of a battle, with plenty to worry about, and be wondering about your fellow solder's sexuality and his ability to be strong and brave? I think, for more than any other reason, gays enter the military to attract more attention to their lifestyle and their movement. They stir the pot and cry for equal rights in the military while demanding to be allowed to act differently. They demand to be taken seriously on the battlefield, but want to be allowed to celebrate their gayness at the same time.

Thanks, Mr. Clinton, for further confusing the whole gay thing. You've sent a message that says, "Enjoy the same freedoms and privileges as anybody else if you're a gay civilian but shut up and hide your sexuality if you're gay and enlist in the military." Either do what common sense dictates and keep homosexuals out of the military, or form a "Gay brigade" where there'd be no question as to who was on the battlefield to fight and who was there to make a political or social statement. (Actually the "Gay brigade" would fit into John Kerry's strategy of fighting sensitive battles, wouldn't it?)

It's ridiculous! It's wrong! It's time to say, "Take this vile crap and shove it back in the closet where it belongs!" If you want to be gay, be gay. But do it in your own home, out of sight, not in public and certainly not in front of my six year-old child. There are more folks that think like we do than there are those who support the gays. Lets act like the majority and quit allowing ourselves to be manipulated and dictated to. We're mainstream America and we're tired of all this Gay stuff!

## CHAPTER 15
# BE PROUD TO BE PROUD

I n our super-sensitive society Americans have been made to feel ashamed of our power and wealth. We have been conditioned to be self-conscious and apologetic of our superior military. Not since we claimed victory in World War II have Americans celebrated our greatness and superiority.

In fact, to call ourselves superior will offend each and every Liberal who has adopted the "Be ashamed of your country" attitude. If Liberals are offended because they feel other countries think we're arrogant, we are! At least we used to be. We used to celebrate our technological, military, moral and societal superiority. We were allowed, and even expected, to be proud of our nation and its accomplishments. The wealth and power America has gained in such a short amount of time is proof of our intelligence, determination and fortitude. Many nations, some that have been around 10 times longer than the United States, are still struggling to provide food and sanitary living conditions for their citizens, while America thrives as a leader in technology and industry, strength and wealth.

Because of our advantage over third world countries, Liberals have devised a plan to act ashamed of our success. This is an effort to make the less successful nations feel better about themselves. By vilifying the accomplishments of a great nation, Liberals voice their disgust of America to suffering nations around the world. By calling America evil because of its strengths and advantages, Liberals try to show other nations they agree with their hatred (see envy) of the U.S. Americans have been conditioned to be ashamed of our accomplishments and achievements. It has never been more obvious that American Liberals are ashamed of our superiority as it was when former Secretary Of State, Madeline (Half-bright) Albright stated that, "America shouldn't be the only superpower in the world." She actually feels that enemy nations should possess the same (or even more advanced) weaponry and tactics than our military has. Good God...who put this woman in a position of power? This would be akin to a heavyweight champ feeling bad about his boxing skills and deciding to fight his next title fight both blindfolded and with just one hand. Makes no sense to me or any other red-blooded American, yet Liberals demand that America voluntarily relinquish any and all advantages we have over other nations in an effort to reduce our capabilities to match theirs. Why not split our military weapons and hardware right down the middle and hand half of it to Iran right now? This "Equality" mentality is a direct reflection of the Liberal's desire to see America fail. What other reason would they have to undermine our power and our strength?

When you hate America it makes sense that you'd want it to fail. In order for this to happen, America must be put on a level playing field with her enemies. This is accomplished by having people like Madeline (Half-bright) Albright and her Liberal friends, publicly denounce America and make apologies to enemy nations for our superiority. This attitude of condemning the achiever and commending the underachievers is apparent not only in Liberal politics, but also in the departments of the infrastructures they are in charge of. Public schools, the news media and the courts are perfect examples of this attitude. Make the strong feel guilty and the weak feel victimized and you have one main component of Liberal theory. They consistently apologize on behalf of the strong and accomplished, while making unbelievable excuses for the weak and underachieved.

This ongoing and consistent outlook has reduced American pride to an all-time low. Americans are on the verge of forgetting that pride of country is healthy, justifiable and should be expected of patriotic Americans. Speaking of patriotic, Hillary Clinton proclaims her patriotism just about every chance she gets. She actually sounds like she's trying to *convince* us of her patriotism. In fact, one might actually think that by publicly performing her rants, she's covering for a complete lack of patriotism. It's obvious that she has no pride in our country and little respect for what our country stands for. She's forgotten the history of our country and the reasons for America's exceptional success. By rewriting history, she and Bill can find justification in belittling our strength and pride and bashing strong and moral leadership.

In fact, Liberals *only* take pride in news that is bad or harmful to our nation. When the economy is good and the stock market is strong, the Liberals are silent. When unemployment rates are low and the job market is strong, Liberals are silent. When our soldiers win battles with few or no American and allied casualties, Liberals are silent. Never do we hear Liberals celebrating positive news or complementing an administration for its successes. Liberals can *only* take pride in the negative. You can't dodge the barrage of coverage from the Left when the stock market dips, the unemployment rate rises or when American soldiers get killed. This is what the Left thrives on… negativity. Hillary blooms in times of "National crisis." The media will only come out from under its rock if it can cover gloom and doom. Condemnations flourish in the Liberal sea of self-loathing each and every time something bad happens to America or its interests. Pride in seeing America damaged or destroyed is the only pride Liberals feel. They condemn anyone who celebrates America's success and demonize those who favor patriotism. These America-hating traitors are the people in charge of destroying Americans pride in country and the idea of loyalty and patriotism. Ironically, they also make national policy from Washington D.C. In the past, traitors that infiltrated our government and worked from the inside to undermine our nation were publicly hanged from the neck until dead. Now we watch them on CNN and ABC news bashing the country and its policies publicly, loudly and daily.

We've allowed Liberals to slowly shape what we tolerate and see as reasonable and acceptable. We're at the point now, that we can't even recognize treason when we witness it every night on the six o'clock news.

Pride in our nation isn't the only condemnable type of pride. In order to make all students equal, pride in scholastic achievements is considered insensitive and rude. You may ask why anyone would condemn a student for being proud of a well deserved good grade or taking pride in being on the honor roll. Unfortunately, Liberals have decided that this pride among hard working students makes their unmotivated, underachieving classmates feel bad about themselves. In order to level the playing field, they dismiss the achievement of good students and concentrate on the "Issues" facing unmotivated ones. It's to the point that Liberals in many school districts around the country want to do away with any grading system that compares one student's achievements against another's. No more A's, B's or C's if the socialists…I'm sorry, Liberals…get their way. We must be made to feel that we're all the same. Any action that offends another, including pride in achieving a good grade in school, must be eliminated. It used to be that a kid that couldn't keep up with the rest of the class was removed and put in a special needs or remedial class so the other students could progress. Now, the entire class progresses at the pace of the slowest student. This allows the slow student to feel good about his or her progress while deliberately denying the more advanced students an opportunity to progress at a more acceptable rate. It's called the dumbing-down of America's youth and it's taking place in every public school classrooms across our nation. Pride on one end seems to lead to poor self-esteem for those on the other end. Therefore, we must eliminate pride to eliminate low self-esteem. That's how the left sees it and it's not limited to our nation's youth.

In today's workplace, being passed up at promotion-time due to ethnic or gender quotas is the reward for pride in a job well done. Our nations professionals and blue-collar workers alike are being slapped in the face for taking pride in doing a job well. Rewards such as bonuses, raises or promotions were once a motivator to insure continued professionalism or production. Workers took pride in their tasks and did them to the very best of their abilities. Their hard work earned them rewards. Conversely, employees in today's work force (many of whom take little pride in their work) expect bonuses and rewards *before* they're willing to work hard and do a good job. It's the entitlement mentality on display again. Unfortunately for those who still have work ethic, and that damnable pride, civil rights and corporate quotas often dictate their advancements. If you're a man, it doesn't matter how hard you work if the supervisory position your working towards must be filled by a woman. If you're a white employee, it doesn't matter how hard you work if that same position must be filled by a minority. Pride in a job well done is systematically being snuffed out by political correctness. I'm just thankful that pride in a job well done is still its own reward for many American workers. You just can't beat the pride out of everyone, can you? Ah, but the Liberals will continue to try.

Then there are immigrants. There's nothing wrong with taking pride in your heritage. Americans from other nations should celebrate their cultures and be proud of the traditions unique to each of their native countries. Just be sure to realize that once you're an American citizen, it's your duty and privilege to *first* celebrate your Americanism.

Liberals prey on the cultural and societal differences among the many ethnicities here from other nations. This creates an atmosphere of separation instead of unity and disassociation instead of community. We can't allow the Left to divide us by nationality and conquer us by pitting ourselves against one another. We must all remember we are Americans first. What is good for one American is good for another and what harms one

American harms another. Pride in America should be as prevalent among American citizens from Germany or France as it is from American citizens from Chile or Samoa. Celebrate what America has granted you and *then* celebrate the customs and traditions of the country from which you came.

If being told to take pride in your newly adopted country is offensive to you, leave now. If you think being asked to show allegiance to America before allegiance to your country of origin is cruel or insensitive, leave now. If you refuse to learn English and become a part of America by respecting American culture and traditions, leave now. Go back to your home because America certainly isn't home to you. America did not become the melding pot of the world by inviting different nationalities into the country only to have them set up small versions of their homelands here. We demanded they assimilate into our communities, learn our language and become Americans. If you want to celebrate your nationality, great. You're now an American Citizen so be proud and stand up for your new home.

The wealthy are another group of people who are demonized and harshly criticized for being successful and having pride in their accomplishments. Liberals love to bash anybody who has a lot of money. "A lot" can mean more than they have, or more than those receiving any form of public assistance, have. These hoarders of money are cruel in the extreme. A millionaire should be ashamed of his excessive wealth, not proud to have achieved the status of"Millionaire." A multi millionaire or (God forbid) a billionaire should just be taken out back and shot for acquiring this level of wealth. This level of financial success is simply offensive and rude to less fortunate individuals. The hard work and sacrifices often required to obtain this level of wealth are dismissed, while the financial rewards for that work are condemned. Poor folks feel bad because they can't afford to drive the same car or live in the same house or wear the same suit as a millionaire. Therefore, millionaires should not be allowed to purchase and own these cars and houses and suits. It's insensitive to those unable to afford them.

Taking pride in owning nice things simply can't be allowed. If rich people continue to be proud of their success, then Liberals will find a way to take their success from them. See "Astronomical taxes" in income, and "Luxury" items. In turn, Liberals find it gratifying to redistribute the wealth they take from the rich, to the underachievers in society.

Liberals find it gratifying to redistribute wealth. This is what Liberals do. They take (through taxes, fees and fines) from the rich and distribute the wealth to the underachievers in society. For some veiled socialistic reason, Liberals feel that those with money should be ashamed, and those without money should be awarded it freely. Here's another example of pride being stripped from those who deserve to be proud.

If America relinquishes its pride and if we continue to cater to the lowest common denominator, we will all become as apologetic and ashamed of ourselves, as are the modern-day Liberals. The America that started as a colony, developed into a stable and respectable nation, fought and won two World Wars, commanded respect with the world's most powerful military and became wealthy and benevolent through a system of free market, will fade into nothingness if Liberals get their way. Removing pride in country is step one in deconstructing our nation. Without pride we can all be convinced to hate our country and badmouth its leaders and practices. Liberalism is like a cancer that, unchecked, will spread negativity and hate to every corner of the nation. Our only hope to stop this is to be proud and be vocal of our pride.

Stand up and cheer the military superiority of the world's most powerful nation. Stand up and cheer the free market that allows unlimited wealth to those willing to work and achieve. Cheer your kids when they receive straight A's on their report card. Celebrate a job well done regardless of the recognition you do or do not receive. Sound off when the stock market hits an all-time high and the jobless rate hits an all time low. Show pride in yourself and pride in your country. Show pride in *being* an American.

And by the way...be sure to tell any self-loathing, America-bashing, gloom and doom Liberal you meet, to kiss you're proud American behind.

## CHAPTER 16
## A TIME AND A PLACE!

This concept used to be taught by parents in the home. Children learned through parental guidance, life lessons and discipline. Unfortunately, today's parents never learned from their parents and therefore, are unable to teach their children the important lessons of "Time and place." The concept of time and place was once considered an important life-lesson and guided our children from childhood into adulthood and then to parenthood.

Like so many other things that have gone by the wayside, time and place is a concept of a bygone day. Along with it go common courtesy, manners, appropriate behavior and common sense. A quick look at our society shows that people have no idea what the concept is.

Lets take a trip through Wal-Mart. Many years ago a shopper might encounter a dog used by a disabled person to guide that individual through the store. Guide dogs and dogs for the deaf, are incredible animals and have an important job to perform. That being said, *pets* have absolutely no business in stores, malls, restaurants, movie theatres, or coffee shops. Wal-Mart is a magnet for rude pet owners who have some sort of separation anxiety and are therefore unable to shop without their pet. Women with tiny rat-like Chihuahua's nestled in their purse, fat guys with a bird on their shoulder, kids with a lizard on their shirt, even an old lady with a cat on a leash frequent our local Wal-Mart as well as other retail stores in my rural town. Common courtesy should dictate that your pet stay at home where it belongs while you are out in public shopping areas. No longer does an individual consider others. If they want to take Rex to the store then by God everybody better be okay with that. When Rex craps in the aisle, there better be an associate available for the "Clean-up on aisle three" call coming across the loudspeaker. And nobody better say a damn thing to me about it because, "Who the hell are they to tell me I can't take my pet in the store with me?" Even the management at many stores allow pets to accompany their owners in order to avoid conflict and lawsuits.

A representative of the Oregon Department of Agriculture told me that in our litigious society, merchants are afraid of being sued by pet owners for banning them from stores. Even grocery stores in my area allow shoppers to bring pets along with them. I'd think this would be considered a huge health violation. Apparently there's a way around that, too.

As long as the animal is referred to as a companion, or an individual claims they are disabled, an animal is to be allowed to accompany them. No proof of their disability is required and neither is any consideration for other shoppers buying groceries. I haven't seen a lot of "Guide-certified" Pot-bellied pigs or iguana lizards, but there they are in the isles at the grocery store. There's not a huge need for ever-pooping "Parrots-for-the-deaf." Yet these animals are becoming more common in coffee shops now. I don't think it's chic, sophisticated or debonair to take your pet shopping with you. I think it's rude and unsanitary.

I think you're rude and I think you should be told as much. If you are unaware of time and place when it comes to sanitation in stores (designated to sell food to the public) you are in desperate need of an immediate education.

Needless to say, a lot of shoppers who are overly attached to their pets don't much care for me. Just like a person who disapproves of the homosexual lifestyle or who disagrees with affirmative action, I'm considered intolerant and close-minded because of my disapproval of pets in stores. I've even been told, "We live in the country. If you don't like it, go to the city and live." I know where the hell I live and I love animals as much as the next guy, but does that give me the right to drag a goat or maybe a cow through the isles at the grocery store? Perhaps I should ride my horse into the local coffee shop and order a sophisticated French coffee concoction. I'm sure that would be okay with the uptight Chihuahua-in-the-purse lady sitting in the corner. I've been told in a fairly snooty way that, "My pet is clean. He goes to the groomer every week." Yea lady, but your groomer can't stop the little fellow from crapping on the floor in front of the produce. Then what happens when a small child comes in contact with the feces? The kid touches his eyes or nose or mouth and there's suddenly a new health hazard where there should never have been one.

The point is, these inconsiderate individuals were never told that taking your pet shopping was unacceptable, rude, or otherwise not allowed. There's a time and place for pets...the grocery store or Wal-Mart is not it. These individuals don't want to hear that they're "Not allowed" to do anything. This includes doing things that common sense tells us we shouldn't do. If storeowners are too frightened to deal with these idiots then it's up to you and me to say something to pet-toting shoppers when we see them. We might even tell the frightened storeowners that they'll lose our business if pets continue to be allowed in their stores.

Not only have we neglected to teach our kids where pets do and don't belong, television is influencing kids by airing shows that celebrate poor behavior and idolize those making poor decisions. Thank you Paris Hilton for dragging your goofy little Chihuahua around with you. It's nice to know that all the dopey teenagers who idolize Ms. Hilton will now know that taking your pet with you, anywhere and everywhere you go, is acceptable behavior. Acceptable, and stylish to boot. Where would our kids be with responsible parents and respectable role models on the tube to reinforce mom and dad's lessons?

I'm not picking on Wal-Mart! I love the place and they usually relieve me of a healthy portion of my paycheck each month. Thought I'd say that before saying this. Wal-Mart is a good place to witness another time and place issue all too common today. Child discipline in the middle of the shampoo isle is unacceptable. Now there's nothing wrong with the occasional "Smack on the hand / behave yourself" reminder if the situation demands it. What I'm referring to is a screaming match between a full grown adult and a spoiled rotten little brat-of-a-kid.

The parent has the kid by one arm swatting his butt as the kid spins in a circle in an effort to outrun the swat. Neither the child *nor* the parent seems to notice they're causing a scene and are attracting the attention of everyone in a five-isle radius. If parents actually did their job of parenting these incidents would not be an issue. Since that doesn't happen, we're stuck with watching the pathetic display while feeling embarrassed for the participants. These public "Whoopin's" introduce another example of the participants not knowing time and place. There's nothing better than the audio to go with the visual when witnessing one of these events.

With numerous *responsible* adults and well-raised children looking on, the parents in these events choose to open their mouth and take the entertainment level up a notch. There's always the gratuitous, "You better shape up you little shit." Or, "I'll whoop yer butt if you don't straighten out." And, the classic, " I didn't raise your ass to act like that, I don't know where you get it." Apparently the use of profanity in public shopping areas is as normal as the "Whoopin'" itself. There's absolutely no concern over who's exposed to it.

While we're on the subject of public family disputes, let's not forget the spousal arguments we're exposed to. Hubby and wife don't have the sense to take the matter home and discuss it behind closed doors. No, they figure, "There's not time like the present." And by God, they have it out right then and there in the restaurant or store or theater. There is simply no concept of time and place.

Kids have a hard time discerning what things are appropriate in the presence of family versus in the presence of friends. When little Johnny farts at the slumber party and his little friends laugh, it's just kids being kids. When little Johnny farts at the table during dinner and everybody starts laughing, it's kind of hard to teach him the meaning of "Appropriate." When little Lisa is allowed to use words like "Crappy" and phrases like, "What the hell," her parents aren't exactly instilling lady-like behavior in their little princess. The language used, and the behavior displayed by today's kids, directly reflect the lack of parenting being done in the home by Mom and Dad. No wonder our youth seem rude and inconsiderate. They simply never learned time and place. These kids grow to be unrefined and are seen as unsophisticated and without any class…which is exactly what they are.

Have you seen our school campuses lately? I'll get to the kids in a minute, but let's start with the teachers. Where were these "Educators" educated? I have very little respect anymore for a group of people who were once admired and revered. On any given day, I can walk onto my son's high school campus and find a majority of the teachers looking like the students in their classrooms. When did every day become casual Friday for our nation's teachers? Hawaiian shirts, cargo shorts, Birkenstocks, faded blue jeans, pocket T-shirts and ball caps have replaced blazers, dress shirts, (or at least a shirt with a collar) ties, slacks and dress shoes.

These same instructors wonder why their students don't treat them with the respect they think they deserve. Their teaching approach is laid back too, and their language in the classroom blends with the speech of the students. "Johnny, that was an awesome story you wrote. It was totally cool how you tied all the characters together." Awesome, totally cool? How old are our teachers and why don't they act their age. Are we paying for our children to be educated by some beach-bum surf rat or by professional instructors certified to teach? Even the administrators are a distorted carbon copy of their counterparts from just fifteen or twenty years ago. Jeans and a polo shirt have replaced the suit and their low standards have replaced the high expectations once placed on our nation's students. Time and place surely isn't being observed in our schools.

Then we get to the students on America's campuses. Obviously the parents of these degenerates have neglected all parenting responsibilities. These kids are completely unaware that they look and act like freaks of nature in what is supposed to be a structured and controlled learning environment. When kids come to class with twenty earrings in each ear, a stud through their tongue, tattoos on their neck, a safety pin through their nose, jet black or blue died hair, baggy jeans hanging around the bottom of their ass, and shirts displaying the middle finger or rude and vulgar quotes…time and place has been forgotten. Is it any wonder we're graduating class after class after class of illiterate, socially inept students? If the purpose of school is to look like a mutant from another world then we're meeting and exceeding our goals. But if school is a place to study, learn and become a well-rounded individual, our nations campuses are failing miserably.

Unfortunately, the lack of common sense in today's society forces our legislators to write and pass laws that should simply be obvious. It forces business owners and companies to place labels and signs where they shouldn't need to be. Take a grocery store for example. "No Shirt, No Shoes, No Service." A rule instituted in order to keep half-naked barefoot people out of the places we shop for food. A good idea that should have been covered by a little common sense. (Yet, for some reason pets are okay.) Why are there signs on the pumps at the gas station that reads, "No Smoking?" Why are there labels on poisons that read, "Keep Away From Children?" Why are there signs at department stores that state, "You Are Being Videotaped?" Why are there warnings on household cleaning products that warn you, "Do Not Ingest?" Why is there a warning on curling irons that reads, "For external use only?" People just don't think!

Folks simply don't think and therefore don't act in an appropriate manner. As a society, we've taken on the responsibility of guarding these folks from injuring themselves or otherwise making bad decisions. I say let them burn themselves in an unintended place with that curling iron a time or two. Let them drink a little Windex or Mop-N-Glow if they want to. It won't take an individual long to learn a lesson if the results of their decision are immediate and unpleasant. In turn, they may tell others of the dangers of making stupid decisions. Word is passed on and viola, before long parents are teaching their kids some basic lessons again.

Simplistic? Of course, but common sense must eventually be re-instilled in our youth by those who raise them. By continuing to protect all ignorant individuals from themselves we're demanding no personal responsibility and without *that* no progress can be made. If we force people to think for themselves, instead of doing their thinking for them, they'll sharpen their thinking skills and improve their decision-making process. As our unrefined youth grow into adults and parents, the next generation is doomed to be just a little more rude, a little less considerate and have an even smaller understanding of time and place.

# CHAPTER 17

# IT'S AMAZING!

There are some truly amazing things taking place in America today. Things I never thought I'd see in my lifetime. Not that these things are amazing in a positive or beneficial sense. Instead, they are actions taken to reaffirm the common sense held by conservatives in America. They're a means of protecting what should never have been threatened in the first place. Unfortunately, Liberals have jeopardized common sense and compromised the values and ideals that shaped America. Let's have a look at some of these amazing things.

## LANGUAGE:

Amazingly, English is now recognized as the official language of America! It's been spoken as the primary language of North America since colonial times. A common language unifies a nation. Multilingualism divides nations. Prior to the colonization of what is now the Eastern United States, scores of Native American languages were spoken in dozens of different regions of North America. Never unified as a nation, Native Americans were separated by language, lifestyle and geological isolation. With the colonization and eventual establishment of America, the United States established a unified country. The Language was English. Individuals were free from religious persecution. Citizens worked for the common good of their community and their young nation. Individuals were proud to be part of such a free and strong nation. Immigrants assimilated to the American lifestyle and immersed themselves in *being* American.

Somewhere along the way, immigrants started to neglect their responsibility to assimilate and become American. Instead, small pockets of minorities formed and grew into small versions of the country from which they came. Many, who still speak their native tongue, never bothered to learn English. Command of the English language should be a requirement of citizenship and mandatory for those in the country for the purpose of earning money. Tourists can get away with broken English but then, they're not here to take advantage of America by making money or becoming citizens.

By allowing numerous languages to become nearly as prevalent as English, America has allowed itself to be put at risk of being divided. If this happens,

America will no longer be America. It will become a land of many nations sharing a common continent. In an effort to re-instill common sense, congress put to vote whether or not English should be considered the "Official language" of America. Amazingly (in today's politically correct-gone-wild society) the vote passed and English was established as the recognized language of the land.

It simply flabbergasts me that lawmakers in our nations capitol had to spend their time and effort to confirm that English was the language of America. Amazing! Remember, "Language diversity" will divide a country. Bad news for America, good news for Liberals! It won't be long before the ruling regarding English, as our national language, will be challenged, deemed unconstitutional and overturned.

## REVERSE DISCRIMINATION:

Some folks are just waking up to the realization that groups like the NAACP and the ACLU promote discrimination and prejudice. Can you believe it? How could a group, formed to advance the progression of "African Americans," ensure equality and advocate for minorities, possibly promote prejudice and racism? It amazes me to think that if the tables were turned, these groups would come unglued and would have more lawsuits filed than they'd have lawyers to handle them.

Let's look at what they get away with…and what the rest of America can't.

It's funny how affirmative action is considered an acceptable practice, so long as it benefits only minorities. I'd like to see the reaction at the ACLU headquarters upon the announcement that a national program to hire and promote White males was being implemented. "We're sorry Mrs. Jackson, you're a delightful employee with an exemplary performance record but the truth is, there simply isn't a spot open right now for an "African-American" woman." "In fact, the promotion is actually going to Mr. Smith in order to meet quota requirements." This would infuriate minority advocates and the likes of Jesse Jackson and the Reverend Al Sharpton. Could you imagine the wrath of the ACLU and groups that work to further "Equal opportunity?" I'd be surprised if the frenzy didn't work itself into riots and violence if ever a "White Male Advancement Program" were to be proposed. Do minorities, who praise the work of these groups, not feel undersold and embarrassed that the color of their skin is being used to facilitate their professional advancement? Black Americans should be insulted that the ACLU and NAACP would overlook their talents, skills and abilities and instead, focus on skin color and "Affirmative action," to further their professional positions. Skin color and race are not a handicap and shouldn't be used to gain advantage over those of different ethnic backgrounds. Yet the NAACP and ACLU act like spotlighting skin color and promoting people based on ethnicity is somehow dignified and fair. In actuality, it cheapens the accomplishments made by those who have educated themselves, strived and excelled in their profession, regardless of Affirmative Action. These groups insult the integrity and intelligence of minorities across the nation by basically saying, "We don't think you're intelligent or talented enough to advance on your own, so we're going to *make* businesses promote you." Unfortunately the idea took hold and now any business unwilling to play along are sued and fingered as a bigoted, racist and evil company. This has been a huge success for the ACLU and NAACP while at the same time it's been degrading and belittling to those promoted based solely on their skin color. Aren't these the very same groups that tell us we shouldn't see a person as Black, White, Yellow or Brown?

Although celebrated among minorities and their angry advocates, "Reverse discrimination" is still discrimination. Isn't discrimination exactly what these angry advocates strive to eradicate? Or have they just been working so hard all these years to simply reverse it? That'll show the evil, bigoted, racist White folks, won't it? They're only hurting those they claim to help.

Good for the goose?:

LOGO, WE and BET! All are cable television stations focused on the entertainment of a very specific group of people. LOGO caters to homosexuals. WE caters to women and BET to the entertainment of

Blacks (although why its not called "African American Entertainment Television," so as not offend anyone with the use of the word "Black," puzzles me.) This is fine with me. After all, most television stations, or at least shows, seek to entertain a target audience. Although this could easily be considered dangerously close to profiling, stations take polls to identify interest and traits in order to identify their target audience. Since profiling doesn't offend me, the use of specific programming on television stations doesn't bug me much either. What amazes me is the hypocrisy demonstrated by those who advocate, promote and watch these audience-specific channels. Let's try a couple of scenarios to see if their tolerance of mainstream America matches the tolerance they expect from you and I.

What would be done to the "Bigots" who started a cable channel called W.E.T. or, "White Entertainment Television?" What if the station's goal was to cater to the interests of only White Americans? Programming documenting the accomplishments of only White athletes, the "Positive influences of the KKK," and how-to shows on minority joke telling would air in the wee morning hours. Mainstream airtime could be used to show films showcasing only White actors doing stereotypically White things. Viewers would know the word "Honky" (or the "H" word,) is slang used only by one White to address another White. The title "Honky" would be highly offensive if used by a Non-White person to address a White individual. I can't imagine the concept of "W.E.T." offending anybody, can you?

Take it a step further and we could launch, "M.E.T.," or Men's Entertainment Television." This could be a channel focused on men-only interests and issues. Commercials addressing the issues of "Masculine itch and odor," and "Male internal issues" would be prominent. Action films would dominate airtime and no movies with any hint of romance or sensitivity would be shown. Porno and hunting shows as well as sports and "Bodily function" contests would fill time slots between bloody feature films. Also, only "Real" men would be permitted to watch M.E. No women, no homosexuals or trans-gender viewers allowed. That may change the name of our new station to "S.M.E." or Straight Men's Entertainment. I don't think it would ruffle any feathers. Do you?

Better yet. Imagine a station called S.O.T.V. (Straight Only Television) that blatantly celebrates heterosexuality and flaunts our morality, family values and happiness in front of audiences' daily. There could be jabs at "Non-breeders" (AKA Homosexuals) to counter their jokes about "Breeders," (AKA us normal folks). The network could promote and host an annual gay-bashing parade then air it repeatedly in an effort to legitimize our behavior. The programming could be used to normalize man-wife relationships and promote the idea that heterosexuals are to be recognized and accepted. Those vocal about their heterosexuality could perform public displays of affection while chanting and holding signs demanding dignity. Also aired on S.O.T.V. could be "Straight Days" at Disneyland, Six Flags and other child-infested theme parks across the country. Straight Days would be a designated day when mass hordes of heterosexuals convene to enjoy the rides while making a statement for morality. Close your eyes, kids.

It just furthers the politically correct concept that as long as *minorities* are being intolerant, or otherwise imposing *their* beliefs on *us*, no criticism of them can be made. Any critic of any minority group is demonized as a bigot and his criticism, however justified, is then tainted by the accusation. Likewise, it is politically incorrect for mainstream America to voice our opinions or beliefs through the same vehicles used by minorities. What they voice is their set of beliefs and it's their right to do so. What we voice is prejudice and racism and therefore we have no right to be heard. By disagreeing with their beliefs, we're accused of spreading intolerance and hate. Is that what we're doing by voicing our support of integrity and values?

## BLAME AMERICA:

What else amazes me? Support for our great nation (or the lack there of) among the American Left. Look at America's response to the attacks that took place on September 11, 2001. For about fifteen minutes

America stood together as one and mourned the loss of innocent American lives. For about fifteen minutes America cursed the terrorists responsible for hijacking commercial planes. For about fifteen minutes America demanded justice for the terrorist acts. For about fifteen minutes we were all angry as hell and were committed to put an end to terrorism on American soil. Then… the Liberals spoke. Out of respect for the dead, they held their tongues for about fifteen minutes. Waiting that long to turn blame on America must have seemed like an eternity to these self-loathing Liberals. Quietly at first, and then louder as the days and weeks passed, Liberals started justifying the terrorist's actions. They blamed the attacks of 9/11 on capitalism and those actively participating in the free market. Since Liberals apologize for the wealth and success of America, it seems strangely logical that they'd turn blame on our prosperity and sympathize with the terrorist. They actually justify the terrorist's actions against the epicenter of our free-market. It's shameful the way Liberals reacted to the attacks. Placing blame on America for the attacks is unacceptable, yet should have been expected.

Following the attacks, President Bush and his administration vowed to locate those responsible and bring them to justice. Already hated by the Left, Mr. Bush was portrayed in the media as a rogue cowboy, bent on revenge and filled with hate. Thankfully, the majority of Americans understand the need for the US to respond to domestic terrorist attacks. We saw what happened when weak leaders like Jimmy Carter and Bill Clinton failed to respond to violence against America. The "Ignore it, and it'll go away" attitude has proven dangerous to our country. Our failure to respond to violence against America and Americans has emboldened our enemies. Indifference has promoted ongoing attacks against our nation's interests. Finally, we had a leader with some balls, who was determined to avenge these attacks on American soil. He was demonized for it. Amazing!

The Left can't get enough when it comes to placing blame on America. When no weapons of mass destruction turned up immediately in Iraq, Liberals rejoiced and reveled in the "Fact" that we were in that country illegally. They sympathized with Saddam when he was removed from power and were appalled that he was photographed when he was finally captured. Saddam's dignity was more important to the Left than were the millions of innocent Iraqi civilians who died at his hands. America was once again to blame for "Invading" a perfectly functional country and removing a perfectly capable leader, simply because George Bush held a grudge. Everything that has taken place in Iraq since the capture of that country's insane leader is the fault of America and its imperialistic ways. The videotaped beheading of Nick Berg and a dozen other captured Americans, the death of more than 3,000 US troops, the killing of innocent Iraqi civilians and the surge of violence in a war-torn country, are all the fault of the United States. And by God, we deserve all the punishment and killing and violence we get.

What else do American Liberals blame America for?

-Global warming.

-The proliferation of nuclear development in rogue nations like Iran and North Korea.

-Endangered species around the globe.

-A perceived lack of financial support of third world countries following natural disasters.

-Instability in the Middle East.

-Racism and prejudice around the globe.

-Poverty and starvation.

-Global pollution.

Liberals who live in America blame all of these problems, and many more, on the United States. These self-loathing apologists simply aren't happy until they've badmouthed our nation and demonized our President. They sympathize with the enemies of America. They commit treason on a regular basis, and then commend themselves on their bravery and courage to speak out against the "Injustices" perpetrated on foreign nations by an evil America.

As I stated before, there are a lot of amazing things going on in America. I just wish that these things were beneficial to our nation. If we'd all just cut the crap and start saying things that need to be said and acting the way we should damn-well be allowed to act, America could once again be a strong, revered and respected nation.

# CONCLUSION

When we step back and look at it, it's pretty obvious that Liberals have been quite successful in implementing their agenda. It's also obvious that America is worse off because of Liberalism.

Political correctness and self-loathing are like cancers. Allowed to go unchecked, they will eventually be the cause of America's demise. We must cut the cancer out. We can do this by neutralizing the Left and rejecting their ridiculous ideas. We can be vocally supportive of those fighting for our nation's safety. We can stand behind leaders who refuse to be victims of terror. We can be optimistic and positive, thus countering the negativism constantly emitted by the Left.

We must regain control of our misguided youth. Parents must parent and children must be taught and disciplined. Without instilling morals, courtesy, common sense, determination and a sense of time and place, America's future looks unstable, at best.

America can remain compassionate when other nations experience disasters, natural or otherwise. At the same time, America must remember that our generosity will not convert our enemies into friends or buy us respect from those who despise us. Support from the American public, not he U.S. government, should be offered to those nations looking to America for relief aid. We are tired of supporting foreign nations with our taxpayer dollars only to be criticized and demonized for not giving enough.

Work hard, show your patriotism, be happy, be proud and above all, *say it like it is*! It's time we quit taking it and start dishing it out. That'll fix just about everything that Liberals have worked so hard to screw up. It's time we quit dropping our jaw every time we're amazed. We must start taking action against all that is counterproductive to America's success and future well-being. Let's preserve the *American* way of life! God bless our troops and God bless America!

# A POEM TO OUR TROOPS...

## By Dave Sampson

You offer up your service to protect our way of life

you proudly sacrifice yourself to preserve our nation's pride.

To you we owe our gratitude and respect for all time

without your service and sacrifice our way of life could not survive.

You put your nation above yourselves and expect so little in return

while Liberals here love nothing more than to see the American flag burn.

You boldly face tyranny, dictators and the like

while back here in America we cry for terrorist's rights.

It's now so damned important that we treat the enemy right

often we forget to protect those who we sent overseas to fight.

So I'd like to say I'm sorry and sincerely apologize

for all the Liberal idiots who do nothing but criticize.

Unfortunately we take for granted our lifestyles and our rights

while all to often forgetting that our rights are won by fights.

So please keep winning battles and killing evil men

and we'll try to remember where our allegiance lies again.

To all the men and women serving in the Unites States Army, Air Force, Navy, Marine Corps, National Guard and Coast Guard...thank you. You commitment to our nation's security and success is admirable and appreciated!

## About the Author

Dave Sampson lives in Southern Oregon with his wife Niki and the youngest of their three children.

Dave grew up in small Southern Oregon towns before attending high school and college in California. Upon returning to Oregon in 1992 he took an interest in the shape our country was taking under the new and disconcerting "Leadership" of the Clinton administration. He has since been critical of Democrats and their leftist amigos, the Liberal Elites. Their efforts to control America and her future are terrifying.

Dave's observations and criticisms of Liberals are poignant and sharp. By pointing out the ridiculous and stating the obvious he inspires thought. His points make you ask yourself, "What is the Left really up to?" Dave uses humor and sarcasm to keep the reader laughing throughout, while at the same time, challenging the reader to see through the veil that Liberals hang in front of their true agendas. A challenge to make every American aware of the danger posed by Liberals in local, state and national politics has inspired him to write common sense political books aimed at all sensible, patriotic, hard-working Americans.

Please enjoy Say It Like It Is.